THE
MUNK
DEBATES
VOLUME ONE

THE
MUNK
DEBATES

VOLUME ONE

INTRODUCTION BY
PETER
MUNK

EDITED BY
RUDYARD GRIFFITHS

ANANSI

This edition published in 2010 by
House of Anansi Press Inc.
110 Spadina Avenue, Suite 801
Toronto, ON, M5V 2K4
Tel. 416-363-4343   Fax 416-363-1017
www.anansi.ca

Distributed in Canada by
HarperCollins Canada Ltd.
1995 Markham Road
Scarborough, ON, M1B 5M8
Toll free tel. 1-800-387-0117

Distributed in the United States by
Publishers Group West
1700 Fourth Street
Berkeley, CA 94710
Toll free tel. 1-800-788-3123

House of Anansi Press is committed to protecting our natural environment.
As part of our efforts, this book is printed on paper that contains 100%
post-consumer recycled fibres, is acid-free, and is processed chlorine-free.

14 13 12 11 10   1 2 3 4 5

Library and Archives Canada Cataloguing in Publication

The Munk debates / edited by Rudyard Griffiths.

ISBN 978-0-88784-248-1

1. Munk debates. I. Griffiths, Rudyard

AS42.M86M86 2010   081   C2010-902472-9

Library of Congress Control Number: 2010932493

Cover design: Bill Douglas
Text design and typesetting: Colleen Wormald

Canada Council
for the Arts

Conseil des Arts
du Canada

ONTARIO ARTS COUNCIL
CONSEIL DES ARTS DE L'ONTARIO

*We acknowledge for their financial support of our publishing program
the Canada Council for the Arts, the Ontario Arts Council, and the
Government of Canada through the Canada Book Fund.*

Printed and bound in Canada

CONTENTS

INTRODUCTION BY PETER MUNK

Since we started the Munk Debates, my wife Melanie and I have been deeply gratified at how quickly they have captured the public's imagination. With our first event at the Royal Ontario Museum in May 2008, we have been able to host what I believe are some of the most exciting public policy debates in Canada; debates that have made a real contribution to the intellectual life of our nation. Global in focus, the Munk Debates have tackled a range of issues such as humanitarian intervention, the effectiveness of foreign aid, the threat of global warming, and the future of health care in Canada and the United States. In the debate transcripts, the reader will have the opportunity to reflect — and in a sense hear first-hand — from some of the keenest minds of our time, debating issues that affect us all. Where else would you have a hard-hitting debate on U.S. foreign policy with Ambassador Richard Holbrooke and Samantha Power taking on Charles Krauthammer and Niall Ferguson? Or hear stimulating arguments about the obligations of rich nations to the developing world, whether in the form of foreign aid or humanitarian intervention, by pitting speakers such as Ambassador John Bolton, General Rick Hillier, Dambisa Moyo, and Hernando de Soto against Paul Collier, Stephen Lewis, Mia Farrow, and Gareth Evans?

Let me say a few words about why we started this program and why we believe so strongly in holding the Munk Debates in Toronto. There are many charitable foundations and worthy causes in Canada. It is part of our national tradition to support public and private charitable initiatives. They form the backbone of Canada's civic life. As a Canadian who wasn't born in this country, a country that has accepted me with open arms and provided me with endless opportunities, I believe strongly that Canada must be a vital participant in world affairs. That was the primary reason that Melanie and I helped found the Munk School of Global Affairs at the University of Toronto, my alma mater. It was the same thinking that led my Aurea Foundation to launch the Munk Debates. We wanted to create a forum that attracts the best minds and debaters to address some of the most important international issues of our time, and make these debates available to the widest possible audience. And we wanted Toronto to be at the centre of this international dialogue to affirm Canada's growing role as a world economic, intellectual, and moral leader. Melanie and I are extremely gratified that the Munk Debates are making significant strides towards fulfilling the mission and spirit of our philanthropy.

The issues raised at the debates have not only fostered

public awareness, they have helped make Canadians more involved and therefore less afraid of the concept of globalization. It's so easy to be inward-looking. It's so easy to be xenophobic. It's so easy to be nationalistic. The hard thing is to go into the unknown. Globalization, to the average Canadian, was an unknown idea. So these debates are meant to contribute to overcoming our fear of further engagement in the world. These debates are meant to help people feel more familiar with the issues, and more comfortable participating in the global dialogue about the issues and events that will shape Canada's future. It is essential today that we equip ourselves, and especially young Canadians, with the skills and knowledge to be vital participants in global affairs. Canada is increasingly a world leader, and we have to assume global responsibilities commensurate with our growing stature.

I don't need to tell you that there are many, many burning issues. Whether you talk about global warming or the plight of extreme poverty, whether you talk about genocide or whether you talk about our shaky global financial order, there are many, many critical issues that matter to people. And it seems to me, and to the Aurea Foundation board members, that the quality of the public dialogue on these critical issues diminishes in direct proportion to the importance, and the number, of these issues clamouring for our attention. By trying to highlight the most important issues at crucial moments in the global conversation, these debates not only profile the ideas and solutions of some of our brightest thinkers and doers, but crystallize public passion and knowledge, helping to tackle some global challenges confronting humankind. Just as important, they seek to make Canada the forum where Canadians and the international community can observe world-class thinkers engage each other on vital matters.

I learned in life — and I'm sure many of you will share this view — that challenges bring out the best in us. I hope you'll also agree that the participants in these debates challenge not only each other, but they challenge us to think clearly and logically about important problems facing the world.

It's easy to come up with ideas about holding debates on this scale. But unless you can execute them, ideas only call attention to what might have been. If this series of debates has succeeded, as a gratifying demand for tickets suggests it has, it is because our organizers, Rudyard Griffiths and Patrick Luciani, have been able to attract great minds and great debaters. We owe a debt of gratitude to them for helping to pull these extraordinary events together. I also want to thank the Aurea Foundation Board for their sage counsel and insights into topics and speakers for our debates. And finally, I want to thank all those who have come out to the live events in Toronto, or to watch them on university campuses across Canada and follow us online. Their enthusiasm validates the Aurea Foundation's vision in launching the Munk Debates four years ago.

Peter Munk
Founder, the Aurea Foundation
Toronto, July 2010

GLOBAL SECURITY

Be it resolved the world is a safer place
with a Republican in the White House.

Pro: Niall Ferguson and Charles Krauthammer
Con: Richard Holbrooke and Samantha Power

May 26, 2008

GLOBAL SECURITY

INTRODUCTION: In the early summer of 2008 it was far from certain that the Democrats under Barack Obama would win the election in November. One of the key issues in that political campaign was national security and whether the Republicans would do a better job of protecting Americans and the West than the Democrats. This debate, which made headlines in the U.S. media, played to an overflow audience of 800-plus at the Royal Ontario Museum in Toronto. As Ambassador Richard Holbrooke said, such a debate, for political reasons, could not have been held in the United States.

Charles Krauthammer argued that a Democratic victory would jeopardize the gains made in Iraq. He reminded the audience of the failed policies under former president Bill Clinton after the attacks on U.S. embassies in Tanzania and Uganda with, as he says, "lobbying of missiles into empty nets in Afghanistan." Holbrooke countered that under President George W. Bush, the Republicans allowed Iran to grow into a major international threat along with North Korea.

Historian Niall Ferguson, an adviser to John McCain during the campaign, reminded everyone that wars were fought under the leadership of both parties. Even President Bill Clinton had authorized the use of American troops against Yugoslavia in Kosovo. But in this case the qualities of McCain as a soldier and successful politician were superior to his opponent's. He argued that it wasn't the party that would protect the West, but which candidate in this election would do a better job.

Samantha Power, an adviser to Obama, made the point that the U.S. under President George W. Bush's leadership had lost credibility to confront China over Tibet and Burma when the U.S. was so indebted to the Chinese. Or the needed UN support for Darfur when America defended water boarding. According to Power, only a Democratic victory could restore international credibility to U.S. foreign policy.

LYSE DOUCET: This debate comes at a time when the Ipsos Reid polling agency tells us that in Canada there's a very deep public malaise about the quality and the quantity of public debating. Even worse, this debate comes at a time when in the United States there is an impassioned debate about politics in every form. So let it be resolved that tonight — here on this inaugural debate, in this magnificent museum — will be the start of a new and more vigorous debate in Canada.

We're going to start on an issue that all of us, no matter where we come from, have to be worried about: the world being a safer place. Would the world be a safer place if a Republican was in the White House? Again, Ipsos Reid posed this question to people in the United States. Fifty-two percent of Americans said the world *would* be safer with a Republican in the White House. However, in Canada only one in four agreed with the statement.

Both sides of the argument would agree that no other president and commander-in-chief could take over the White House at a more difficult time. The next president of the United States will be challenged to restore American respect, American moral legitimacy, to win over friends, and to decide how to deal with foes.

First for the motion, Niall Ferguson.

NIALL FERGUSON: Thank you very much, Lyse, and thank you, ladies and gentlemen. As all Scotsmen have Canadian relatives, I knew entirely what to expect when I came here this evening. My uncle, aunt, and cousins warned me that trying to defend the Republican Party in Ontario was a suicide mission straight out of the Pacific War.

However, it seems to me that there is a case to be made for this motion. As an historian I find the idea that over the last hundred years Democrats have consistently made the world safer than Republicans implausible. A moment's reflection on the history of the United States will set the record straight. All the major wars fought by the United States in the twentieth century were fought by Democratic and not Republican presidents. It's easy to forget that even under that great peacenik Bill Clinton, the United States took military action in three different countries, and when it took Kosovo it was far from clear that it was within the scope of international law.

But I'm not going to weary you with a history lecture because this motion isn't really about Republicans; it's about *that* Republican, John McCain. It seems to me that this distinction will make a significant difference to this debate.

I wouldn't be standing here talking to you now if any of the other potential candidates for the Republican nomination had been voted in. Providentially, the Republicans nominated the one man who is ideally suited to lead the United States out of the legitimacy crisis, the diplomatic crisis, and the military crisis in which it finds itself. John McCain is a man with an extraordinary record: twenty-two years as a serving naval officer. Five and a half of those years were spent as a prisoner of war, and his spirit was unbroken by that experience. He has received seventeen military honours, and served twenty-six years as a legislator, twenty-two of them as a senator. The word "experience" matters in this debate.

The notion that John McCain is somehow too old for the presidency is easily dismissed. Relative to the median age of other American presidents, he is by far not the oldest president in modern times. In fact, nine other presidents in the past hundred years have entered the White House older in relative terms than John McCain will be when he becomes president at the age of seventy-two.

But it's not just his experience that is relevant here. The thing that most impresses me about John McCain is that he understands the predicament that the United States finds itself in. He sees that there is no way that the United States can walk away from Iraq with the job unfinished, half finished, completely aborted. The stakes are too high. This is not 1968; this is not Indochina. We are talking about the most strategically vital region of the world, and the United States cannot afford to allow that region to descend into a maelstrom of sectarian violence and geopolitical conflict. Whereas a year or two ago many people feared that the ultimate outcome of the American invasion of Iraq would be a catastrophe, today the surge has proved those Cassandras wrong. John McCain took an enormous risk when he backed General [David] Petraeus's strategy to increase troop numbers in the region; it very nearly cost him the nomination. But John McCain is not a man who's afraid to take that kind of political risk.

At the end of 2006, the monthly fatality rate in Iraq was running around 4,000; it is now around 500. There is a realistic prospect that the situation in the country will be stabilized. There is also a realistic prospect of the Iranians being driven out of the south. This is not fantasy; this is fact. It is contrary to the expectations of Barack Obama but speaks very well of John McCain's military judgement that, although he had repeatedly criticized the way in which the Bush administration handled the Iraq crisis, he saw that an increase in troop numbers was the only possible way in which that situation could be brought under some kind of control.

But this election isn't just about Iraq. In fact, I think with every passing week it may become less and less about foreign policy and more and more about economic policy, and I just want to remind you that this is an unusual state of affairs. It's not every day that the most important economy in the world goes into a presidential election during a recession, and with a realistic prospect that the domestic situation could deteriorate further. The question is, what do these candidates have to say about our economic safety and security? Only one candidate for the presidency is clear about the need to avoid raising taxes and raising federal expenditure at a time of recession, and is clear about the importance of free trade. Let's not forget that Senator Barack Obama was not unwilling to stoop to a sideswipe against NAFTA in his pursuit of a few extra votes. It is extremely important for Canada — and indeed for the rest of the world — that the leader of the United States should have an unshakable commitment to free trade. We need a straight-talking president in the United States. We do not need the heir to Jimmy Carter, which is what I fear we could get. We do, however, need the heir to Ronald Reagan. Thank you.

LYSE DOUCET: Thank you, Niall Ferguson. Samantha Power, against the motion.

SAMANTHA POWER: Let me start by echoing what Niall has said about John McCain. John McCain is the most honourable, the most experienced, and the most knowledgeable of the Republicans in the field. First, a Republican president would continue a war in Iraq that has left the U.S. military at its breaking point, undermining U.S. military readiness — which in turn undermines the United States' ability to concentrate resources in Afghanistan, a place that Canadians have a deep interest and invested interest in stabilizing. Also, that undermining of military readiness interferes with the United States' ability to engage in the strategic lift of peacekeepers from the developing world to places like Darfur.

Second, a Republican president will continue a war in Iraq, and policies associated with that war would undermine the United States' ability to lead within international institutions on a range of other issues, from the hard security issues, such as nuclear proliferation or the containment of Iran, to Darfur and Burma. Even when the United States does change its foreign policy, as I think Senator McCain is prepared to do in some measure on the issue of climate change, our summoning power in the United Nations and in global bodies and regional institutions will have been undermined.

Thirdly, a Republican president, specifically President McCain, will spark an overdue internal debate about the role of torture in American foreign policy, a practice that has not only deep moral and legal implications, but profound national security implications. And here I quote none other than U.S. Secretary of Defense Donald Rumsfeld's famous standard whether the war on terrorism was working. As you recall, the question he posed was: "Are we capturing, killing or deterring and dissuading more terrorists every day than the madrassas and the radical clerics are recruiting . . . ?" And here, of course, because of Abu Ghraib and Bagram and Guantanamo, the answer is no.

Now, as many of you know, the honourable John McCain has pledged to reverse most of the egregious excesses of the Bush administration — to close Guantanamo, to return the United States to the Geneva Conventions. But will John

McCain, who has shown very worrying signs of playing to his base, be prepared to convene a 9/11–style commission to establish meaningful accountability on the issue of systematic torture and systematic abuses as part of U.S. detention policies? McCain, who's been well out in front of his Republican colleagues on this issue for obvious personal and I think deeply held moral reasons, recently sided with the majority of Republicans in the Congress in seeking to exempt the CIA from U.S. military rules of interrogation and engagement — military rules that are much more in line with international law. That's a worrying sign.

Fourth, you can expect a Republican president will continue to uphold the policies of non-engagement in the realm of diplomacy with America's adversaries in the Middle East. And given the fact that stability in Iraq depends fundamentally on a regional solution and regional involvement, this is deeply worrying.

Now I'd like to say something about Iraq and Iran, the two issues that Niall has also suggested will divide the candidates, Senator Obama and Senator Clinton on the one hand and Senator McCain on the other. First, on the issue of Iraq, you will hear an awful much this evening about the cost, and I want to say at the outset that these costs absolutely have to be considered. We have to do everything in our power to mitigate the cost in terms of the al Qaeda presence that has come to Iraq in the wake of the U.S. invasion — and, crucially, but too often left out of the domestic debate in the United States, the fate of Iraqis who have relied upon the promise of the American presence, many of whom have recoiled against that presence but all of whose destinies have been forever altered by that same presence. Consideration of human consequences in discussions of withdrawal is essential.

You will hear much dogma about the inevitable effects of a U.S. withdrawal, and I think it's worth remembering that the same people who will warn you dogmatically about the coming apocalypse are the same people who argued that American soldiers would be greeted with flowers and chocolates as liberators. John McCain himself said in September 2002, "We're not going to have house-to-house fighting in Baghdad; we're not going to have a bloodletting of trading American bodies for Iraqi bodies." In January 2003, two months before the war, he said, "We will win this easily." I'm not saying that this means that the warnings of harm to civilians or the warnings of Iraq can be discounted, as some progressives seem inclined to do. But one has to be careful about dogmatism in the realm of national security, especially in the wake of the recent record.

So the costs of withdrawal have to be taken into account. I hope in this discussion we can talk about how to mitigate the harms associated with departure. But there is no acknowledgement, or very little acknowledgement, of the cost of staying, and we cannot look at Iraq in an *à la carte* fashion. We must look at the cost of staying to U.S. soldiers; to the recruitment of terrorists, both in the context of detainee policies and the occupation itself; the cost to Afghanistan and stability there; and, crucially, the cost to U.S. summoning power. When you look at public opinion polls about the United States, it's tempting to view them simply as popularity contests — that is how they are parodied in certain circles in the U.S. But they are a measure of America's ability to get what it wants in international institutions. It matters when you have a 5 percent approval rating in a country. Governments fear they will fall if they affiliate with the United States on crucial issues, and in the context of Iran. I think it is reckless at this stage not to embark upon every policy that we can in service of stability and in service of the mitigation that is suffering. That does not mean that you meet with an abusive regime, a holocaust denier, tomorrow. But it does mean that ruling out aggressive diplomatic engagement is reckless — precisely the kind of recklessness we've seen over the last seven years. Thank you.

LYSE DOUCET: Now, for the motion, Charles Krauthammer.

CHARLES KRAUTHAMMER: Thank you, Lyse. I'm sometimes asked to compare what I do today as a political analyst in Washington with what I did twenty-five years ago as a psychiatrist in Boston. I tell people, as you can imagine, that it's really not that different. In both lines of work I deal on a daily basis with people who suffer from paranoia and delusions of grandeur, except that in Washington they have access to nuclear weapons, which makes the work a little more interesting because it raises the stakes.

Ladies and gentlemen, the stakes are very high in the 2008 U.S. presidential election. That's why we're here to debate whether it would be better for the world, for the safety of the world, if a Republican or a Democrat were elected. And let me say that if the Democrat running for president were

Harry Truman, I would be on the other side of this debate. But the former vice-presidential candidate for the Democratic party in the year 2000 said plaintively and with regret that the Democrats have abandoned the tradition of Roosevelt and Truman and Kennedy, who said in his inaugural address that America would pay any price, bear any burden, meet any hardships, support any friend, oppose any foe in order to ensure the success and survival of liberty. Senator Joe Lieberman said he is the last Truman Democrat, and ostracized as he is from his own party, he chose to support John McCain as president because he sees McCain as the best guarantor of the security of the United States, and by extension of the safety of the world.

Both the Democratic candidates and the Republican candidates have insisted that the single most important foreign affairs issue that the American people should choose a president on is the war in Iraq. As the Democrats have made extremely clear in their debates and in their statements, there is a stark difference between the two positions.

The position of Hillary Clinton and Barack Obama is unequivocal. On the day they are inaugurated as president, they will call in the Joint Chiefs of Staff and ask them to immediately prepare a plan for the evacuation of Iraq. Obama says the withdrawal will take place over sixteen months, but he will begin to remove combat troops almost immediately. The position of John McCain is diametrically opposed. On the day McCain is inaugurated, he will bring into his office the Joint Chiefs of Staff and ask them to provide a plan to try to achieve success in Iraq. And by success I would refer to what General David Petraeus said in his testimony last week to Congress: he defines success in Iraq as an Iraq that is at peace with itself and its neighbours, an ally in the war on terror, and with a government that serves all Iraqis.

In 2006, when the war in Iraq was at its lowest ebb, America had essentially lost its way; the Democrats concluded that the war was lost. They said so, the majority leader in the Senate said so, the House Speaker said the war is lost. The Democrats ran an off-year election pledging to withdraw American troops unconditionally, regardless of conditions on the ground, and they won a smashing electoral victory. Ever since then their position has remained unshaken — that is the position of the party, the position of their leaders, and the position of the President of the United States if a Democrat is elected. The problem is that the situation on the ground has changed in the last two years, and the Democrats refuse to accept the empirical evidence of the astonishing changes on the ground in Iraq.

Essentially, when al Qaeda had conquered Anbar Province, a secret CIA report at the time had declared Anbar lost. Al Qaeda has since been driven out of Anbar, and the Sunnis have changed sides in the civil war, and joined with the United States. There are 80,000 Sunni civilians who are on joint neighbourhood patrols, armed and supported by the United States. Al Qaeda is on the run. Its last redoubt is in Mosul, and the Iraqi army has launched a campaign in Mosul against the organization. This is an extremely important event in the war on terror.

We did not seek a war with al Qaeda and Iraq. But al Qaeda had decided that after the fall of Saddam Hussein, they had an opportunity to strike at the United States and declare Iraq as the central front in the war on terror. It was their understanding that the war in Iraq would be the great challenge to the United States, and for a year and a half it looked as if they were succeeding. They are now on the run. If America stops, as the Democrats advocate, if they give up the war and allow al Qaeda to reestablish themselves in Anbar, in Baghdad, and elsewhere, it will be a catastrophic defeat for the United States and the world, taken out of the jaws of victory.

Al Qaeda is now at the point where, if it were defeated, as it is on the way to being defeated in Iraq, it will be a humiliation for Osama bin Laden and his cohorts. They have declared Iraq the central war front, recruited Sunnis, co-religionists, and co-sectarians aggrieved against the United States. And they will have witnessed their own co-religionist joining with the infidel against them and defeating them.

That is an extremely important event in the war on terror. Iraq would be entirely in jeopardy were America to withdraw, and, as a collateral effect, the central government, which is the one hope for a reasonable democratic representative government in the region struggling to establish itself, would collapse. Abandoning Iraq would not only lead to a humanitarian disaster, it would be a strategic catastrophe, self-inflicted unnecessarily, and that's why America must elect John McCain, who will not allow that to happen.

LYSE DOUCET: Now against the motion, Ambassador Richard Holbrooke.

RICHARD HOLBROOKE: I am honoured to be part of this panel with my friend and colleague Samantha Power. She and I are supporting different candidates in the primaries, but we will be united behind the Democratic nominee. We also share our firm opposition to this resolution, which we're debating tonight.

I'm also pleased to debate such worthy antagonists as Charles Krauthammer, the author of the famous 1990 article on foreign affairs, which proclaimed the post–Cold War era was America's unipolar moment. Things seemed not to work out as precisely as he predicted. And Niall Ferguson, a man for all seasons, whom I hope, trust, and expect will see the error of his ways next year when the Democrats will listen to their critics. And I speak as someone who served every Democratic president from Kennedy on. We take seriously what other people say, unlike the current administration.

The question before the house tonight is simple: Is the world a safer place with a Republican in the White House? Based on the record of the last seven years, our opponents tonight want you to believe that, having weakened the United States throughout the world, their party should be given another chance. One of the two bases his position solely on the fact that he's behind John McCain, or he wouldn't be here tonight. The other says he would only be on the other side if the Democrat were Harry Truman. Charles, regarding Harry Truman, if he were running today, he'd be even older than McCain. The current administration has done nothing on climate change, and they have mismanaged Afghanistan, an internationally supported effort in which Canada has borne a disproportionate burden.

When I was in Afghanistan last month, NATO commander General [Dan] McNeill went out of his way to praise

Canada, and I commend the bipartisan efforts of the Canadian government to extend their participation to 2012. But in order to be worthy of your confidence, the United States and its allies must change its strategy in Afghanistan.

The Bush administration has allowed Iran to grow into a major international threat. They've watched North Korea go from one nuclear weapon to six to ten, based on the estimates. They have watched and presided over a long, steady decline in America's standing throughout most of the world, from our allies to our adversaries. They have allowed America to be defined by the most abhorrent events. Words that have entered the English language in the international lexicon as shorthands for something that does not represent our great nation: Abu Ghraib, Guantanamo, torture. This administration openly opposed the bills banning torture in the Congress, and presided over a spectacular decline in the strength of the dollar and the weakening of our economic position internationally. They've done far too little to deal with dictators in desperate places such as Burma, Zimbabwe, Sudan, and elsewhere — and you'll notice I haven't yet mentioned Iraq.

The Republican argument is quite simple. It's based entirely on fear. Fear of the Democrats, misrepresentations of their past, and misrepresentations of their current positions. They say, "We have messed up Iraq so far, but we can't let the Democrats take over because they'll make it worse." That is the core of the two arguments you've heard from my distinguished colleagues. Yet all they offer is more of the same, particularly when it comes to Iraq. I do want to note, however, that Senator McCain is the only Republican who has said that climate change is an important issue and, therefore, will be a major change in his policy.

Although the candidates do differ on important details, on the key issue that Charles Krauthammer has focused on, Iraq, there are tremendous differences. In my view, Iraq will be the defining issue of this election. I respectfully do not agree with Niall that the main issue during this election will be the economy, for a simple political reason: those people who will vote based on the economy have already made up their mind, and that will favour the Democrats. The undecided voters will be faced with exactly the choice Charles posed, although I respectfully disagree with his conclusions.

Now here is what the two Democrats still standing — Senator Hillary Clinton and Senator Barack Obama — have said: both say that they will withdraw combat troops in an orderly and careful manner shortly after taking office. The Pentagon says this would take twelve to sixteen months at a minimum, given the difficulty. You can't go through Basra anymore, which is being taken over by the Iranians. And let's be clear on that: Iran is taking over Basra, though it's unreported by the press. So the troops will have to get out by air through Turkey. It will be very difficult, so it will be done very carefully.

Neither of the two Democratic candidates have given a certain date for full withdrawal of all American military personnel in Iraq, notwithstanding the impression of deliberateness put forward by our two worthy opponents. Both have said that if it's the right thing to do, they would leave an unspecified residual presence to deal with the very terrorist problem that Charles Krauthammer referred to — a problem which he neglected to mention did not exist before the invasion of Iraq and which was caused by the chaos created by the policy he so strongly supported. Both Senator Clinton and Senator Obama have said, "Put Iraq in a regional contest and bring in the neighbours." The bad news is that one of those neighbours is Iran. But to settle and stabilize Iraq you must have a political solution. You can't do it militarily, and this political effort has never been seriously tried by the Bush administration.

LYSE DOUCET: Thank you. So Iraq is the defining issue. General Petraeus, probably the best person to tell us what's happening in Iraq, describes the situation there so far as fragile and reversible. Charles Krauthammer has already declared victory: astonishing success, astonishing changes. Niall Ferguson, the same: the surge has proved the Cassandras wrong. It's sort of McCain-esque declaring victory in Iraq.

CHARLES KRAUTHAMMER: That is a lovely misrepresentation of our position.

LYSE DOUCET: "Astonishing changes" — I quote you, Charles Krauthammer.

CHARLES KRAUTHAMMER: The changes are astonishing because no one anticipated that al Qaeda would be driven out of Anbar.

LYSE DOUCET: And into the Diyala Province and Baghdad.

CHARLES KRAUTHAMMER: Al Qaeda is not in Diyala or Baghdad; they're in Mosul. Now, astonishing changes have occurred, and it is precisely because they are fragile and precisely because they are reversible. The idea of withdrawing on a timetable, regardless of conditions on the ground, is a prescription for disaster. The difference between the Democrats and McCain is that McCain says he wants to try and entertain withdrawals, but only on conditions that meet our requirements, only if conditions on the ground allow it, *because* the situation is reversible and fragile. It is precisely because there is not a *fait accompli* that we have not declared victory. The difference between now and 2006 is that in 2006 you could have plausibly argued that the war was either lost or unwinnable; you cannot plausibly argue either side right now. The Democrats have persisted in a policy based on the assumption that it is easier lost or unwinnable, and they are impervious to the empirical evidence to the contrary.

LYSE DOUCET: Well, why is it that John McCain seems to be the only Vietnam War veteran in the Senate who has reached the conclusion that you can win this war, that by sending in more troops and staying longer the United States and its allies ultimately prevail?

NIALL FERGUSON: This actually illustrates a critical issue, namely that McCain has consistently underskewed the character of this war. There was no house-to-house fighting in Baghdad; it was exactly as he foresaw. In 2004, he said there are not enough troops in Iraq, and we're going to lose control. In 2005, he was extremely critical of the way Donald Rumsfeld was handling the situation. One of the points that McCain has made is that we have already tried troop reductions, and the results were absolutely calamitous. When we brought the troop levels back up at the end of 2005, the violence dropped, just as McCain predicted, and I don't think "astonishing" is the wrong word. Look at the data from the Brookings Institute. The monthly death toll, as a result of troop reductions, went up to four thousand fatalities. From four thousand to a thousand casualties a month is a major breakthrough. That is not defeat, and in that sense I think McCain has been consistently right.

LYSE DOUCET: You know Senator Obama well, Samantha Power. When was the last time Obama was in Baghdad?

SAMANTHA POWER: 2006.

LYSE DOUCET: He doesn't go there a lot, though; John McCain has been there many times, Hillary Clinton has been there many times. If Iraq is the supreme challenge, why should we entrust the future of Iraq to him?

SAMANTHA POWER: Obama is the only mainstream candidate — and certainly the only candidate left in the race — who opposed the war in Iraq back in October 2002. If you go back to his speech in October 2002, it is not filled with anti-war jargon, nor is it the statement of some ideologue trying to pander to a progressive sector of the purple state of Illinois. Obama actually foresaw the difficulties, very much unlike John McCain — who did say, Niall, we will win the war easily two months before the war began.

LYSE DOUCET: But Obama doesn't seem to have any faith at all in the military side of the equation in Iraq, and it is clear the U.S. military presence in Iraq is having an impact. Barack Obama doesn't even want to talk about the positive impact of the military presence in Iraq. If he becomes Commander-in-Chief, he's going to immediately withdraw troops from Iraq, which some people would say is precipitous.

SAMANTHA POWER: He has never said precipitous withdrawal. Obama was the first person to say President Pervez Musharraf is an unreliable partner. We're giving the country a billion dollars of aid without asking where the assistance is going. A lot of it is being used against their own people — the very secular, moderate forces that we want to see prosper in Pakistan. He got Iraq right. He was the first person to say, "We want to open up our relationships with Cuba. At some point is there a statute of limitations on a failed policy?" There are a series of judgements and evidence that he does not "focus group" his way to policy decisions in the way that other candidates do.

Now to your second question, which is whether or not Obama understates the value of military force. I don't think he does at all. Obama is prepared to leave a residual force in Iraq to deal with al Qaeda. He doesn't believe that al Qaeda will simply vanish into thin air in the absence of a U.S. troop presence. It's unclear where that force will be based and how large it will be. He is somebody who has never taken military force off the table with regard to Iran's nuclear ambitions. He is somebody who has said that if President Pervez Musharraf is unable or unwilling to deal with al Qaeda in the northwestern provinces of Pakistan, the United States will have to go after them. Senator Obama looks across a range of national security challenges, and does not see the military as the only tool in a vast American foreign policy toolbox.

RICHARD HOLBROOKE: I want to address the issue of dialogue with Iran. This is a huge issue. President George W. Bush initially said he would not talk to either North Korea or Iran. As a result, the North Koreans made a significant increase to their nuclear arsenal. He reversed this policy under advisement from Secretary of State Condoleezza Rice in 2006 and began a six-party dialogue, the other parties being China, Russia, the two Koreas, and Japan. He put a skilled professional diplomat in charge, Ambassador Christopher Hill, and as a result of that dialogue some progress has been made. Some people didn't think it was enough, and interestingly President Bush's major critics are former members of his own administration on the right, such as John Bolton, who have called the six-party talk a sell-out. Nonetheless, the North Koreans turned over more than 18,000 pages of documents on their acquisition and use of plutonium to the United States last week. Those documents are now being analyzed by the intelligence community, and based on that judgement, the president will decide whether to proceed down the road towards progress with North Korea.

On the other hand, Bush has still done nothing with regard to Iran. He still insists on talking to Tehran through two channels, neither of which fills the needs that I mentioned in my earlier statement. First, and most important, is Iran's very dangerous nuclear program. The United States speaks to Tehran through the EU's foreign policy representative, Javier Solana, who carries messages back and forth between Washington and Tehran. Now many of you in this room are distinguished diplomats — David Wright, who was ambassador to NATO from Canada; political writer Alan Gottlieb. You all know Javier Solana — he's a good man, but why would the greatest and most powerful nation on Earth think that they are strengthening their position by sending their message to Tehran through a European diplomat who has a different style of negotiating and may not accurately convey our position?

The second channel is at the ambassador level in Baghdad, where Ambassador [Ryan] Crocker is political counsellor and has an intermittent dialogue with the Iranians about their outrageous, murderous behaviour in fuelling bomb attacks and road mines against Americans.

That's not a dialogue, and the position of the Republicans, including at least one of our worthy opponents here, says that any talk at all would be a sign of weakness. It is simply not true that negotiations or discussions in and of themselves represent weakness. Weakness is conveyed inside the dialogue and not as a result of talking to people.

NIALL FERGUSON: With all due respect to Richard, there's no point in talking for talking's sake to a rival power, which is in a position of such obvious strength. The critical thing that happened when the United States opened up dialogue with China was that China's position had been fundamentally altered strategically by the breakdown of its relations with the Soviet Union. That is what opened the opportunity for President Richard Nixon. There is no comparable situation today; nothing has changed. Economically, Iran has difficulties. Domestically, Iran is by no means as anti-American as other countries in the region. There is a potential for some kind of transformation in relations between the U.S. and Iran, but it won't happen if Barack Obama hops on a plane, hoping to be welcomed with open arms. That's not how diplomacy works.

LYSE DOUCET: But if seven years of doing it the Bush way didn't work, why should more years of McCain doing it the same way work?

NIALL FERGUSON: The reality is that the option of using force against Iran needs to be credible. If the Iranians pursue their nuclear arms program, which the International Atomic Energy Agency today says they show no sign of abandoning, the United States cannot say, "We only want to talk; we won't bomb you, we promise." That's why the parallel I drew a moment ago with the president and China is interesting. It wasn't a Democrat who made that single most important departure in American Cold War foreign policy. It was a Republican. Why? Because Richard Nixon had the credibility to open up dialogue in a way that in my view only John McCain has. I certainly don't think Barack Obama has a snowball's chance in hell of opening up dialogue with Tehran. The Iranians will be celebrating if he is elected.

RICHARD HOLBROOKE: Niall makes an important political point. It's easier for somebody on a conservative side to reach out to the other side. But Niall, let me remind you that it was a Republican president — Ronald Reagan, the hero of the Republicans — who sent his National Security Advisor to Tehran with a cake with a key in it. Let's not forget which administration reached out to Tehran in a humiliating and disgraceful way. The core issue is that Senator McCain has not taken the position Niall has outlined. Charles has been notably silent because, as suggested earlier, I do not believe he shares the view we just heard.

CHARLES KRAUTHAMMER: Well, my silence was a sign of politeness, but now that it's been misinterpreted I retract my silence and I shall speak to this issue. This whole argument about speaking with Iran or the others is ridiculous. In our history, you sometimes speak with enemies, you sometimes don't. It depends on the conditions. Obama says he was asked, "Would you be willing to meet separately and without preconditions during the first year of your administration in Washington with the leaders of Iran, Syria, Venezuela, Cuba, and North Korea?" He said, "Not only would I, but the fact that the Bush administration refuses to do something comparable is a disgrace and ridiculous." Now I think this was an off-the-cuff gaffe. He was not prepared to answer that question, and now he's stuck with what he said. Then you go through the eighteen months of preparation as [Henry] Kissinger did, and you try to negotiate an agreement in advance so that the communiqué is basically written by the time the president arrives. But the idea that a president in his first year will meet with the leader of Iran and other rogue nations without preconditions is absurd. That does not mean you don't have back-channel contacts. It does not mean that we don't have the British and the French and the Germans negotiating on our behalf as they have for three years.

The reason that summits are dangerous is because once you hold a summit everybody expects a result. There's pressure to have a result, and results are a result of concessions. What concessions have the Iranians offered? None. What concessions will Obama offer in return to entice them? Does he believe that his eloquence alone will induce Iran to give up its nuclear ambitions?

LYSE DOUCET: I want to get to Samantha Power, because the point made by Charles is one that actually Hillary Clinton made by describing Obama as "naive;" John McCain described him as "naive" and "reckless."

SAMANTHA POWER: First of all, I think Charles has the question correct, and had the answer correct when Obama said "I would," but then he changed it to, "I would be willing, conceivably, to meet within the first year." Obama has at no point said, "I pledge to meet, unconditionally, with President Mahmoud Ahmadinejad." What he has said is that if it would advance U.S. interests, he is open to the possibility of dialogue, and it is irresponsible when U.S. lives are on the line in Iraq and Iran has such a major role to play in the region to rule that possibly out. It's not the same as saying you're going to meet without preparation or you're not going to think pragmatically about what a negotiation achieves — the upsides and downsides, both of which could be considerable.

Threatening the use of military force against Iran, which both Senator McCain and the current administration have done repeatedly, has done nothing to deter the enrichment of uranium, which is now occurring at five times the pace. It has however, strengthened Ahmadinejad's hand domestically. I mean, Niall, your rosy picture of Iran notwithstanding, I would think that this would concern you.

Finally, when the United States has gone to other countries and said, "We need to contain Iran, this enrichment intelligence is deeply worrying," most of the world leaders have basically yawned. You cannot have a containment regime in the multi-polar world we live in. The United States is the only country that believes what it's saying about the threat that Iran poses. *Negotiating*, not a meeting for meeting's sake; areas of overlap where you could conceivably make progress or remind the world that Iran is the problem and the United States is not.

CHARLES KRAUTHAMMER: The correct answer to the question "Would you meet unconditionally with these rogues as president?" is a simple no. That's not the answer Obama gave, and now we have Samantha and the others who have to clean up after him saying, "Well, really we're going to meet, not with preconditions, you have to understand, but with preparations." So the word "preparation" is going to become a substitute to try to undo the mistake he made with "preconditions." A president does not meet unconditionally, without condition. A president does not go and shake hands with Ahmadinejad without precondition. That's the right answer. Hillary gave the right answer in that context, McCain wouldn't think twice, and Obama obviously was unprepared and he stumbled and now we're stuck with it.

LYSE DOUCET: We had a discussion about Barack Obama. Help us, Niall and Charles, to understand John McCain.

NIALL FERGUSON: Well, I think there's no question that in McCain you see two streams of foreign policy tradition, realism and idealism, coming together. The idea that you could have a league of democracies as a complement to existing institutions in the international system is obviously idealistic. In fact I'm sure Richard would acknowledge that it's one that has its antecedence in the Clinton era, but at the same time — and more importantly — John McCain understands that such ideals can only be viable if they are based on a credible constellation of forces.

That is why, if you look at John McCain's *Foreign Affairs* article from the end of 2007, or his most recent speech in which he said, "These are the things I want to look back on in 2013 that I've achieved," he makes it very clear that diplomacy, effectively directed, particularly at Russia and China, will play an integral part in his foreign policy. Diplomacy was not regarded by George W. Bush or by Donald Rumsfeld as necessary for the überpower that the United States had become. John McCain sees statecraft and diplomacy as central foreign policy tools, and only after those have failed to get the Russians and the Chinese to recognize the need to contain Iran's nuclear ambitions will there be any consideration of military options. That's the difference between McCain and Bush; and it's also the difference between McCain and Obama.

LYSE DOUCET: You mentioned the league of democracies. You say it's a complement to existing institutions in the international system, but some people say a league of democracies allows the United States to fly in the face of multilateralism and go around the United Nations, which doesn't include China.

NIALL FERGUSON: Well, the United Nations does not have a tremendously impressive record on acting on humanitarian catastrophes. In recent interviews, John McCain has said that if we're to take any action to stop the genocide in Darfur, it will have to be through some kind of coalition of democracies — because it's clear that the Chinese don't give a damn about human rights in Sudan, or in their own country for that matter.

RICHARD HOLBROOKE: As Niall had already said, this idea exists today. It was put into place by Bill Clinton in 1998, and their headquarters are in Warsaw. The Bush administration refused to touch the league of democracies because it had Clinton's fingerprints on it and the people advocating it were all liberal Democrats. I'm delighted John McCain joined that cause.

Let me say a word about John McCain, whom I've known for twenty years and consider a friend. There are many areas of agreement between John McCain and both Democrats. Hillary Clinton and John McCain serve on the Armed Services Committee, they travel together, they like each other, and it is alleged that they've even had a drink or two together in places like Estonia.

But I want to stress that there are wide areas of agreement. All of us on this panel believe that the United States must regain its leadership role in the world; if we don't, the world suffers. My own view is that we want leadership without hegemony, but the Bush administration has offered hegemony without leadership. I do not disagree that McCain is the least bad of the nine candidates the Republican electorate were offered. The defining issue is Iraq. The issue of the United Nations and the league of democracies is a very difficult subject. Many share the feeling that the UN is a negative factor in world affairs. The fact is that the United States and a few of our allies, including Canada, created the UN in 1945 to solve a set of problems. The key to the UN and the context that we're talking about today is the Security Council, in which we gave ourselves a veto to protect our interests. We've used that veto more than all the other four countries that have right of veto combined, and we've used it for a variety of reasons.

From day one, the Bush administration undermined and underfunded the UN. It also appointed as one of the ambassadors a man who declared that the UN wasn't an organization that was fit to exist, by proposing reforms that he knew were impossible to achieve.

I was an ambassador at the UN for several years. It is a deeply flawed institution. However, we are still better off with it than without it. Our job is to improve the UN, to break down the iron lock of the so-called G7. I know the developing countries think the UN is a punching bag and a way of getting money and leverage. But when the UN won't act — as it wouldn't act in Kosovo — we, together with the Canadians and our NATO allies, went around the UN, liberated the Kosovo Albanians in 1999 with seventy-eight days of NATO bombing, and then went back to the UN and got everyone, including the Russians, to agree to what we'd done.

That's what we have to do with the UN. We have to make it better, not undermine it. I'm all for the league of democracies, but I do not think, as Senator McCain has suggested, that it can substitute for the UN. Even our closest allies, including Canada, will not agree to that proposal.

LYSE DOUCET: Let's bring it back to leadership. John McCain feels the league of democracies is a useful forum. He's said that if there was a league of democracies, it could impose sanctions on Sudan and force Sudan to accept peacekeeping troops. Charles, what does this tell us about the kind of leadership John McCain would show?

CHARLES KRAUTHAMMER: I've been in favour of a league of democracies for a long time. The UN is useless, counterproductive, injurious. It's almost a fiction. A league of democracies would undo the mistake we made sixty years ago, imagining that universal international institutions are the way to go. "Universal" includes rogue states such as Russia and China, both of which stopped action in Sudan, Darfur, and elsewhere. Nothing ought to be expected from the

United Nations, and the idea that the Bush administration's inadequacies are the reason the UN has been ineffective is ridiculous. The UN is inherently dysfunctional because it was established as a coalition of the winning states after the Second World War. Within a year the member countries were at odds with each other, and that paralysis has lasted sixty years. If you want to act multilaterally in the world, then you establish a league of democracies with the understanding that over time you would hope it would displace the UN. Americans are too emotionally attached to the idea of the UN to ever withdraw from it, which is why I think a league of democracies is a clever way to dispatch the UN, without ever withdrawing. But I want to say that when Lyse was earlier speaking of John McCain, and said dismissively that he was for the rollback of rogue states —

LYSE DOUCET: I wasn't dismissing, I quoted him.

CHARLES KRAUTHAMMER: You quoted in a way that there was a note of skepticism, and I find this astonishing. What's wrong with a rollback of rogue states? Canada is a country that is distinguished in its history for having invented peace-keeping, having devoted itself to international institutions to bring peace into the world's most troubled areas.

The United States has taken action in Iraq against the second worst man on the planet — a man who had committed genocide on his own people; a man who used weapons of mass destruction, and chemical attacks on innocent civilians; a man who had committed the greatest ecological crime in history by dumping 400 million gallons of crude oil after the Gulf War into the Arabian Gulf and the Persian Gulf to keep U.S. forces from coming ashore. This is a man who drained the swamps in southern Iraq in order to starve and destroy the marsh Arabs, an ecological and human rights catastrophe of the first order. The United States acted to depose a dictator and bring democracy to Iraq's citizens. You can argue that the United States have mismanaged the occupation, and I would agree, but to question the United States for having undertaken an action that I would imagine Canada, with its long history, would applaud for the nobility of its objectives is to me astonishing. If you can roll back a rogue state, you ought to do it in the name of humanity.

SAMANTHA POWER: First of all, Niall and Charles, go back to Rwanda, which is the greatest emblem of UN failure.

CHARLES KRAUTHAMMER: And the United States under the presidency of Bill Clinton —

SAMANTHA POWER: Well, this is my point. It was the *Belgians*, a democracy, who withdrew at the first sign of casualties. It was the United States, under President Clinton, who went to the UN Security Council and insisted on the withdrawal of peacekeepers from under General Roméo Dallaire. Why? Because the United States was afraid that if the peacekeepers stayed, the U.S. would somehow be called upon to act.

The only countries currently willing to send peacekeepers to Darfur as part of a UN force were authorized to do so because of belated high-level diplomatic pressure on China, which finally acquiesced in the importance of a peacekeeping force. The only countries that put boots on the ground in Darfur are developing countries, and most of them are not fully democratic nations.

The central problem of creating an alliance of democracies is that democracies fundamentally are not interested in bearing the collective security burden of the planet right now. I think focusing on institutions is an alibi to dealing with these humanitarian challenges. You could create as many new institutions as you want, but unless you change the political priorities of these places, you're not going to get anywhere. Think about the central challenges on the rise in the twenty-first century: global warming and terrorism. The very countries that we need counter-terrorism and intelligence co-operation from are countries that are not democratic.

We've got to deal with the polarization that is tearing this planet apart right now, and we can do it bilaterally, but the more international legitimacy you have, the more you can pool resources from countries that don't see their entire national interest at stake.

Right now there are a hundred and seventeen thousand peacekeepers active in the world, and around twenty-one missions. All but two or three thousand of those troops are from non-Western countries. To think that it is only the developing world that is dealing with major humanitarian calamities is really to pass the buck.

CHARLES KRAUTHAMMER: The reason that hundreds of thousands died in Rwanda was not because of institutional deficiencies or that the Belgians did not step up. It was that the United States did nothing. Are you willing to support an American invasion of Darfur? If the answer is no, then you're not serious; if the answer is yes, then let's do it. We saved hundreds of thousands of Iraqi citizens who had been slaughtered by Saddam Hussein for more than a decade, and all we get from critics is that it was a war for oil. It was a war about Abu Ghraib. It was a war of liberation exactly comparable to what you want to do — or at least imply what you want to do — in Sudan. If there's a country that will move the world it has to be the United States, given its strength and capacity. And if you're serious about that you want to advocate more intervention, and not less.

SAMANTHA POWER: Do I support a U.S. invasion of Darfur? I do not, and I'll tell you why not. There's plenty of things the United States can do in order to ensure that twenty-six thousand peacekeepers get deployed to Darfur within six months and that will allow the two million people in refugee camps to live tomorrow. Do I support U.S. invasion? No. Why? Because one sector of the American society is bearing the entire national security burden. The military is broken; we don't have the readiness to respond to anything that hits us on our own shores.

Would I be in favour of waging a third war in eight years against an Islamic country? No, because it would undermine the U.S.'s national security interest and the interest of the refugees. The only thing worse than the atrocities being perpetrated against people in Darfur is when you combine atrocity and jihad and inflict upon the people in Darfur what we have inflicted upon the people of Iraq.

CHARLES KRAUTHAMMER: I'm not in favour of another invasion, but unless one believes that the United States is willing to act and that America is justified in acting, I can't see how you can be serious about protecting the people of Darfur. Just a few days ago new trouble has erupted in southern Sudan because of the discovery of oil there. If you want to be serious about Sudan, which is protected by China, you have to be willing to act seriously.

LYSE DOUCET: Niall, you advised John McCain on foreign policy. How would you advise John McCain on China?

NIALL FERGUSON: It's extremely difficult for the United States to contemplate any kind of unilateral or even multilateral military intervention now in Sudan. That's partly because the military is overstretched, and that's why John McCain very sensibly argues that one of the things that he would do as president is to increase the size of American military forces. But the critical point here is to ask ourselves about the shape of the strategic world to come.

Let's look ahead. At the moment it's Africa you worry about, because the population growth is creating a Malthusian crisis there. In a forty- to fifty-year time frame, it is China. China is scrambling for natural resources in sub-Saharan Africa, and the effects of their presence in Africa will pose a major challenge to the strategic security of not just the United States, but all developed economies.

We need a president who understands these geopolitical shifts of power, and who realizes how high the stakes are going to be in the next four to eight years. This is the new world. Arguments about who was right and who was wrong over the invasion of Iraq are in some ways irrelevant. The clash over commodities is as big an issue as the world has ever confronted, and I don't hear any credible answers to the question of how the United States will deal with these challenges from Barack Obama. John McCain, on the other hand, is very clear. He sees the strategic ambition of China in the Far East, just as he understands the way in which Russia is using its energy power to intimidate our allies in Western Europe. These are the issues that are really going to be critical in this next presidency. You cannot afford to have a novice dealing with issues of this importance.

LYSE DOUCET: I'm going to pose a question from the audience. Richard, I'll direct this to you. "Mr. Obama wants to talk, but this is a tough world. Can he throw a punch if need be?"

RICHARD HOLBROOKE: Based on Senator Obama's extraordinarily skilful campaign, I think the answer is self-evidently yes — and I speak as a person supporting Senator Clinton. He's run a terrific campaign tactically and strategically, and he's shown that he's tough enough to dish it out with senior Democrats. Now he's taking on McCain one on one, and it's very impressive. Is he tough enough to be president? Yes. Anyone who survives the presidential marathon ought to be tough enough, unless they happen to have won by one vote in the Supreme Court and their father was president.

I want to make a quick comment on Darfur. Samantha's right, nobody's advocating U.S. troops on the ground for all the reasons she said and many more. But the United States proudly led the fourteen-to-nothing (China–abstaining) resolution in the Security Council that was going to send peacekeepers to Darfur, after which we did nothing to implement it. Each time someone asked the president why we weren't doing anything in Darfur, his answer was "It's the UN's fault, they don't have any helicopters." They need maybe twenty-five helicopters. We could supply them, and there are many other things we could do. Final point, I find it ironic that you would instruct Samantha, who wrote the definitive book on Rwanda, about the Clinton administration's failure to act in that region. As a person who served President Clinton with pride, I can tell you that it was a low point of the administration.

CHARLES KRAUTHAMMER: The point I wanted to make is not a partisan point. It is to say that those who care about these humanitarian crises have to step up and be serious. Pushing it off on institutions like the UN, which have been proven ineffective time and again, or on peacekeepers who often are corrupt and involved in rape and other criminal activity, which is even more horrific than the diseases it's trying to cure, is a serious mistake. I'm not in favour of invading any nation. I'm saying if you're serious about peacekeeping, show us and make a case.

LYSE DOUCET: We have another question from the audience: "To what do you attribute the kind of emotional appeal that Senator Obama exerts on people all over the Western world?"

CHARLES KRAUTHAMMER: I think Senator Obama's appeal is remarkable and a tribute to his astonishing skills — his intellectual nimbleness, his attractiveness, and his ability to rise from obscurity in three or four years to dominate the American scene. I would attribute all of those qualities and achievements largely to him. There is of course another element. America has been looking for a long time to atone for one of its greatest sins, which is without a doubt slavery, Jim Crow, and racism. When Colin Powell was flirting with the idea of running for the presidency in the 1990s, there was a tremendous outpouring of support. I think many people in America would love to see a vindication of the civil rights revolution, and in some way an expiation of our sins in the past, by having an African-American as president. I know I would like to see the United States reach a point where an African-American is president of the United States. The question, of course, is which African-American? Thomas Sowell, an economist and philosopher and one of the most astute writers in America, who himself is African-American, raised that issue in a column just a few weeks ago. He said he would support someone of his race if they were the kind of person who reflected his values. People have talked about race being an issue in the campaign, and obviously it is. There's a finite number of Americans who would not support a black candidate. I think there's also a finite number of Americans who would like to support a black candidate, all things being equal. I'm not sure which of those numbers is the larger, but I would hope and expect that the latter is a larger number, and I think it would be a great thing for America. The fact that Senator Obama is the front-runner in this campaign is going to raise that issue front and centre, and I hope that we'll come out of this election with a healthier understanding and perception about race in America than we did at the beginning.

LYSE DOUCET: We have a question from the floor from the Deputy Leader of the Liberal Party of Canada, Michael Ignatieff.

MICHAEL IGNATIEFF: This is a question for the Republican side. You have raised the issue of moral seriousness and you've raised the issue of humanitarian intervention, and you've said if you're serious about Sudan you should go. What I'm unclear about is the principles that John McCain, or the Republican side, would use to decide when and where and how to intervene when there's ethnic cleansing, genocidal massacre, or — as we've recently seen — a regime like Burma forbidding the entry of food aid, resulting in the starvation of its citizens. What are your criteria for intervention?

NIALL FERGUSON: John McCain was recently asked the same question by Matt Bai from the *New York Times Magazine*, and he gave, I thought, a very thoughtful reply. He made it clear that the United States could not randomly or universally intervene in humanitarian catastrophes because of the crucial need to have the support of the American electorate for action taken involving the lives of American troops. The American electorate is not about to become a global cop intervening in any country whose leaders are performing horrendous acts against its population. That would be a

completely unrealistic and utopian project. National interest has to be a factor, and public legitimacy has to be a factor. I think John McCain understands that there is no other
way in which a responsible and experienced politician could
make that kind of decision. You have written about this
subject as eloquently as anybody I know, and have grap-
pled with this fundamental dilemma of democratic politics
over the last decade in a way which I've found profoundly
influential and moving. We do empathize with the plight of
the people of Zimbabwe, a country not mentioned this evening. We, I hope, feel abhorrence towards Robert Mugabe's
authentically evil tyranny in that country. But can we
credibly imagine any American president, regardless of
his partisan allegiance, sending troops into that country
to be accused, as he inevitably would be, of a neo-colonial
project? This is a difficult thing. Humanitarian intervention calls for judgement on a case-by-case basis, and I think
John McCain has shown clearly he understands that.

RICHARD HOLBROOKE: I want to point out the facts of Zimbabwe, which by the way I did mention. President Bush went to
Johannesburg and stood next to Thabo Mbeki and said, "We
will talk to Mugabe through you." That's not leadership. We
all know that, only yesterday, President Mbeki did suggest
for the first time that maybe things in Zimbabwe weren't
going so well. He did that because he suddenly discovered
that the Zimbabwe refugees are destabilizing South Africa,
which everyone knew was going to happen. So let's get the
facts straight here.

No one is advocating military interventions in Zimbabwe.

But it is the inability of this administration to know how to put together meaningful coalitions using existing international organizations that is the problem. That is the problem in Darfur, where you talk about the Chinese, and I completely agree with you about the Chinese, but they have changed under pressure. Who did that pressure come from? Washington? No — Mia Farrow. She had more effect in Darfur than the United States government.

Mia Farrow wrote an article in the *Wall Street Journal* about how supporting China as host of the Olympics in Beijing would be tantamount to supporting genocide in Darfur. Right after, director Steven Spielberg withdrew as the adviser for the opening ceremonies, and within three weeks the Chinese appointed a special envoy who came to see me in New York. I'm not making a point about Mia Farrow: I'm making a point about the administration's lack of understanding. I'm responding to the points both you and Charles made about the administration's diplomatic incompetence on all these issues. You just cited Zimbabwe and Darfur. I believe Senator McCain will be a better president if he's elected than the incumbent — I don't disagree with you on that point. It is Iraq that is the real voting issue. Collective action through existing international institutions is the key. Every nation in the UN voted for military intervention in Zimbabwe, and it wasn't implemented. The U.S. has made no effort to lead a coalition to implement a resolution it helped draft.

CHARLES KRAUTHAMMER: You say that Mia Farrow writes an article and as a result China sends a special envoy to talk with you, but how many people have been saying "Darfur" as a result of that piece?

RICHARD HOLBROOKE: That's because there's been no U.S. government backup. The point is that international public civic action pressure, which Samantha has been a central part of, has had more of an effect on Beijing than Washington. That's the core point.

LYSE DOUCET: You both keep coming back to the centrality of Iraq as a deciding factor in the upcoming presidential election. But one issue that Canadians are worried about is what's happening in Afghanistan. Do you see a problem with maintaining forces in Iraq when many are saying the same thing about Afghanistan?

NIALL FERGUSON: Well, I do think the situation in Afghanistan is as important as the one in Iraq, though you would never guess that from the lack of coverage of Afghanistan in the U.S. media. There is a degree of stress and strain on the U.S. military and on the militaries of NATO allies, and that is precisely why John McCain has turned his attention to the question of how quickly we can improve our military capability. At some level it's very simple: it's about numbers. The United States did not have enough combat troops to successfully execute the national security strategy that it embarked on in 2002. That doesn't mean that the strategy was wrong; it means that the means were not there. But I just want to take up a point that Richard has just raised. Seventy-five to 80 percent of the things that Richard Holbrooke has said tonight would have been relevant if we had been debating the re-election of George W. Bush. Bush cannot stand for re-election, so his record is kind of irrelevant.

RICHARD HOLBROOKE: Not as long as McCain defends it.

CHARLES KRAUTHAMMER: I find it interesting that Richard brings up the difficulties in Afghanistan as an argument *against* a Republican administration. Let's remember what Afghanistan was in the 1990s. The attacks on the United States that came out of Afghanistan in the name of al Qaeda happened under the Clinton administration. What happened after the attack on our embassies in Tanzania and Kenya? The lobbying of missiles into empty tents in the deserts of Afghanistan. What happened after an American warship, the *Cole*, was attacked? A classic definition of an act of war. The Clinton administration responded by sending FBI agents into Yemen to apprehend the perpetrators.

That lack of response exposes the Democrats' fundamental misunderstanding of the conflict in the war on terror, on the nature of the conflict with al Qaeda. The Democrats understood terrorism as an issue of law enforcement. When the World Trade Center was first attacked in 1993, what was the Clinton administration's response? To put a couple of miscreants on trial. President Clinton put the perpetrators in jail and thought that had actually addressed the problem. The current Attorney General of the United States, Michael Mukasey, happened to have been the presiding judge in that trial, and not only was it a complete distraction from the war on terror, but Mukasey will tell you that because we granted the rights of ordinary Americans to these terrorists in open trial, al Qaeda learned about our intelligence from them. They learned from an open discovery process that we had been listening in on Osama bin Laden's communication by satellite phone, and that phone was shut down within a day. When we compare the beauty of the world in the year 2000 — when the Democrats left — with our difficulties today, our opposition here is ignoring a central fact: 9/11 happened; 9/11 was an unprovoked declaration of war on the United States, which occurred during a Republican administration and which changed the world. The Bush administration had to respond to the attacks. From the ground up, the Bush administration devised an entirely new strategy of addressing an enemy which had up to that point been ignored because it had been seen as a criminal problem, as a law enforcement problem in the previous decade. The Bush administration created a new set of institutions to adapt to that war. When 9/11 occurred there wasn't anybody in Washington or anybody in any administration — Democratic or Republican — who imagined that we would go another six months, or even a year or two, without a second attack. The fact that we have not had a second attack in six and a half years is not an accident. It's not because al Qaeda had decided to unilaterally disarm. It's not because al Qaeda accepted Jeffersonian principles of democracy. It's because the United States confronted al Qaeda on the ground in Afghanistan, today in Iraq, and established institutions that have prevented a second attack. That will be the legacy of the Bush administration.

LYSE DOUCET: Let's take another question from the floor. Pamela Wallin, former Consul General to New York.

PAMELA WALLIN: Is there a way in the short term for America to move troops into Afghanistan? How do you deal with that, because as we learned in Iraq, time is of the essence, and if there's not a movement of a greater number of troops in Afghanistan, then I think that poses a problem. The other issue is related to the security of both of our countries, and it was raised earlier on the question of energy resources.

RICHARD HOLBROOKE: We're now in the seventh year of this war in Afghanistan. It is that war that we must win. Whatever happens in Iraq, the war in Afghanistan will go on a lot longer than the war in Iraq. The Taliban cannot win. You can't win based on terror tactics, such as executing teachers in schools because their students are young girls. The memories of the black years in Afghanistan make the overwhelming majority of Afghan citizens not want the Taliban to succeed. However, having said that the Taliban can't win, I must say with great regret that the side we're supporting cannot win either, as it is currently operating. In other words, we have a very dangerous long-term stalemate. What are the factors that must be addressed?

First, the Pakistan border. We now have an Afghan-Pakistan theatre of war. NATO forces can fight only on the western half of it; we can't go into Pakistan, except briefly, covertly — a predator drone here, a few nighttime raids there, because of the politics of the situation. The new Pakistani government is involved in negotiations that may result in giving them more breathing room against the militants and putting more pressure on Afghanistan to contain al Qaeda.

Second, the drug situation. The drug policies that the United States has followed in Afghanistan are without doubt the worst foreign assistance program I've ever seen in my forty-plus years in and out of service in the U.S. government. Last year the U.S. alone spent eight hundred million dollars on drug eradication. It isn't just a complete waste of money; it is helping the enemy. According to its own statistics, for the eight hundred million dollars the United States invested in drug eradication, it got a 40 percent increase in opium traffic last year.

The third thing is the weakness of the government. Afghanistan's government is corrupt, it is weak, and within that subset the police are even worse. This is the most important issue that we haven't addressed. These problems must be fixed. There are a dozen other problems — the role of women, agriculture — but those are the four I'd single out: the border areas, drugs, corruption of the government, and the total hopelessness of the national police force. This administration has done a very bad job on addressing these issues when they should have done better for all the reasons we know.

I agree with Niall that I'm attacking this administration too much, partly because Senator McCain has not clearly laid out his position on Afghanistan yet. I hope we will change our position on Afghanistan next year because we can't afford to lose this war.

LYSE DOUCET: Thank you, Richard. Now on to a very important issue for Canada: NAFTA. When they were campaigning in Ohio, both Senator Obama and Senator Clinton said they'd reopen it.

SAMANTHA POWER: Obama has long talked about some of the benefits of free trade. His concern is the people who have been hurt by NAFTA and the impacts on environmental labour standards. He looks forward, I am told, to sitting down with Canada and Mexico and looking at environmental and labour standards. He has been fully supportive of — and he has voted for the Peru free trade agreement, and he has voted against the Colombian one because he felt there were insufficient provisions. He is not anti-trade. He is just looking to strengthen those measures.

LYSE DOUCET: And that brings us to a close on this part of the debate. Let's give our four fine debaters another chance to convince you of their arguments. Three minutes each, starting with you, Richard Holbrooke.

RICHARD HOLBROOKE: First of all, I want to thank Peter Munk and CBC for this opportunity. I sure hope there are debates of this quality and intensity in the United States to inform its voting public. I thought a great deal about Senator McCain's central argument, which is if you get out of Iraq things will get worse, and the Obama/Clinton argument that we have to start to draw down our combat troops. This is an enormously difficult decision, and I believe it will define the next presidency.

Unlike our Republican colleagues, I am not filled with certainty about the war in Iraq, and I'm astonished at their certainty, given their track record over the last seven years. It is the toughest problem I have ever seen in my government service, and with all due respect I am the only person here who has served under combat in the United States government on several continents. I've negotiated with the worst people in the world; I work closely with the Canadian government and other governments, trying to improve the condition of humanity; and I've also worked heavily in Africa on issues such as HIV/AIDS. So I care passionately about these issues.

It is my view that the McCain/Bush position on Iraq boils down to this: stay there forever until we win. Neither of our opponents have addressed the amount of time the McCain strategy would require in order to achieve success. Stay there forever in order to avoid defeat? That means people are going to die — coalition forces, Iraqis, civilians — if we don't create a process that stabilizes the region. First, that to me raises fundamental problems of morality. Second, it's going to drain the United States of the capacity to deal with all the other problems of the world. One last thing: we haven't had time to talk about China and Africa, and, by the way, it's not China and Africa — it's China. Africa's just a leading edge. But I think the other side has inaccurately and inadvertently diminished the climate change issue. There is plenty of room for leadership on that issue, and thank God you have a Republican candidate who agrees with that particular point.

LYSE DOUCET: Thank you. Charles?

CHARLES KRAUTHAMMER: I want to also thank you for the forum, for the opportunity to address you in this remarkably interesting political year in the United States. The issue of NAFTA was raised, and I think you have to understand as Canadians that it is a symptom of a larger issue for the Democrats. They are now in a period of withdrawal, pulling in on protectionism, appealing to the popular sentiments of a people who are economically dissatisfied and weary of a war abroad in another long twilight struggle. The appeal to protectionism is not an accident; it's a part of the drawing in.

It seems to me extremely odd that a leading candidate for the presidency would make a point of scapegoating NAFTA and Canada in a time of economic difficulty. It's extremely odd that Obama would say that he would take the hammer to Canada on NAFTA and at the same time say he's going to have a chat with Ahmadinejad, given the fact that Canada has been an incredibly stalwart and courageous ally in the war on terror in Afghanistan. As many Americans, Republican and Democrat, are aware, Canada has the highest per capita casualties in the war on terror. And as an American who was raised, nurtured, and educated in Canada, that does not surprise me because I know of Canada's history in the twentieth century, the courage and valour its soldiers displayed in the First and the Second World Wars — which, incidentally, Canada entered long before the United States. I find it rather odd and unfortunate that Canada should be used as a scapegoat. But America is drawing in as a result of this long twilight struggle.

Richard is right, no one is certain about an outcome in Iraq. But one thing is certain: if we liquidate the war the way the Democrats want, we will have a return of al Qaeda; we will have a collapse of the government in Baghdad; and possibly even have a genocide, which our opponents here are so concerned about in other areas of the world. So I say the safer course is to elect a man who understands the difficulties of this issue, who's been in combat himself, who understands the military, who has experience and has a realistic understanding of what has occurred on the ground and how the peace ought to be preserved. Fragile it is, delicate it is, reversible it is, and that's precisely why it cannot be allowed to be reversed. Thank you very much.

LYSE DOUCET: Thank you, Charles. Samantha.

SAMANTHA POWER: Charles said something very important about Darfur. One could generalize in terms of American foreign policy or even in terms of Canadian foreign policy. Those who care must, as he put it, "step up and be serious." We probably all agree with that, but it is clear that we have very different perspectives on what "stepping up" and "being serious" entails. We had a long discussion about Iraq, we had a long discussion about Iran, we talked about Darfur, we talked about Afghanistan, we talked about fixing the UN, we touched upon trade. All of these issues — in a globalized world where everyone can see all policies at once, and the policy statements of leaders in Western countries are broadcast into countries where economic and security interests are at stake — are connected, and we have to see those connections and talk and think about policies that are responsive to those connections.

I think stepping up and being serious entails recognizing those connections, and I want to give you just a few examples. Our standing in the Middle East, our ability to broker or be useful in helping broker an Arab-Israeli peace agreement, will be affected by how we get out of Iraq or how we draw down in Iraq. Again, the struggle against terrorism and the proliferation of terrorism will be affected in terms of how al Qaeda's residual presence in Iraq is dealt with. An important point is that Sunni tribal chiefs have done more of late to contest al Qaeda in Iraq, and we should hope that continues. And both Democratic candidates are for maintaining a residual force. But this connectivity goes further. You cannot do as the Bush administration has done — and I know John McCain will not do it, but it's a temptation to call on UN forces to be sent to Darfur, then denounce genocide on a Monday; to endorse water boarding on a Tuesday, and then turn back on the United Nations on Wednesday, and expect other countries to take you seriously.

It is very difficult to put meaningful pressure on China in the context of Burma, Tibet, and Darfur when China has become America's ATM machine, which is what has happened over the course of the last seven years. It is very difficult to build a coalition in Africa that will have credibility with Robert Mugabe on the issue of democracy in elections when we back Pervez Musharraf — uncritically — in Pakistan. We have got to understand that dealing with multinational threats — global threats — are going to require actually being able to summon and not simply coerce co-operation. Thank you.

LYSE DOUCET: Thank you, Samantha. And last but not least, Niall.

NIALL FERGUSON: Ladies and gentlemen, I want to remind you of something: this is your only chance to vote in this election, so please use your vote wisely. We need a president who knows war; we need a president in Washington who knows torture. Samantha completely misrepresented John McCain's position on torture. He has led the way in condemning the maltreatment of prisoners of war. We need a president who understands what Richard seems to have overlooked: that giving up in Iraq could end up costing many more lives. We need a president who can command respect from allies and a measure of fear in our enemies. We need a president who's not afraid to do the right thing, even when it means being unpopular. We need a president who has learned from history that you don't just sit down with the bad guys without preconditions. We desperately need at this time — when trade barriers are being raised all over the world, not least because of rising food prices — a president who is committed unequivocally to free trade, and is not afraid to say that free trade has created many more jobs in the United States than it has lost. We need a president who understands the magnitude of the challenges that the United States and the Western world faces from a renascent, rapidly growing Chinese dragon, and an incorrigible Russian bear.

One final point that's been unmentioned this evening: we need a president who realizes that the war on terror is not over. Experts put the probability of a nuclear attack on an America city at somewhere in the region of 15 percent. Think about that. Al Qaeda has expressly said that its intention is to carry out a Super 9/11. Ladies and gentlemen, it has to or it's finished. It's failed in Iraq, and 9/11 did not bring capitalism to its knees. What do you think they are going to do next? I ask a question that was asked quite rightly by Richard Holbrooke's friend Hillary Clinton: Who do you want to answer that telephone at three in the morning? Thank you very much.

LYSE DOUCET: Niall Ferguson, Charles Krauthammer, Richard Holbrooke, and Samantha Power. Join me in thanking all of them.

SUMMARY: The audience voted 29 percent in favour of the resolution at the beginning of the debate. At the end, 46 percent voted in favour of the resolution and winning the debate.

HUMANITARIAN INTERVENTION

Be it resolved that if countries
such as Sudan, Zimbabwe, and Burma
will not end their man-made humanitarian crises,
the international community should.

Pro: Gareth Evans and Mia Farrow
Con: John Bolton and Rick Hillier

December 1, 2008

HUMANITARIAN INTERVENTION

INTRODUCTION: Few topics evoke more emotions than that of humanitarian intervention — history is full of examples of the tragedy of non-intervention. But whether intervening will always help or whether it is even always possible was at issue when four debaters — Americans Mia Farrow and John Bolton, Australian Gareth Evans, and Canadian Rick Hillier — debated the following resolution: Be it resolved if countries such as Sudan, Zimbabwe, and Burma will not end their man-made humanitarian crises, the international community should.

The pro side found actress and activist (in particular on the matter of Darfur) Farrow and Australia's former Foreign Minister and President and Chief Executive of the International Crisis Group Gareth Evans paired up, while the con side featured the United States former Permanent Representative to the United Nations and former Under Secretary of State for Arms Control John Bolton and Canada's Rick

Hillier, former Chief of the Defence Staff, the highest position in the Canadian Forces.

Farrow spoke passionately about her experiences in Darfur and of her belief that it would be possible to help in the region without putting Western troops in harm's way. This proved to be the main point of division in the debate, for while everyone concurred that it would be desirable to help, Bolton emphasized that an "international force" actually means an "American force," and Hillier asked the audience to imagine how they would react once the casualties started mounting. He used his experiences in Afghanistan as proof of how fickle public support can be for a mission, regardless of how dire the crisis.

BRIAN STEWART: It is an honour to take the reins of this debate. Humanitarian intervention is an inescapable problem for reporters, for diplomats, for soldiers, for voluntary groups working in the field, indeed for all of us. The same questions keep coming up: when to act, when not to act, what action would work, what action might make the situation worse.

Governments do ask and wonder — does the public really care enough? Will the public care even in the face of casualties? I learned a long time ago that these questions do get asked because humanitarian interventions have mixed results, as we know.

Take, for example, the civil war in Somalia in the early 1990s. It seemed for a while it would be easy to put a cap on the militias that were interfering with humanitarian work there. Three years later, the United Nations had to retreat, and chaos has existed in Somalia ever since.

And there was the genocide in Rwanda. Eight hundred thousand lives may have been saved had there been intervention beforehand. The genocide remains an open sore — it is a terrible problem for Africa, the region around it, and the world.

The war in the Balkans was long and arduous, but would you not consider the UN and NATO intervention in Bosnia a success?

The mission in Afghanistan was not undertaken as a mission of humanitarian intervention, but more as an international security intervention. It has morphed increasingly into a latter-stage humanitarian crisis, thus raising the question: does one stay for the long haul or leave?

A few years ago, after the genocides in Rwanda and Srebrenica, the United Nations put forth the Responsibility to Protect doctrine, or R2P. It is a doctrine that declares that if a state cannot or will not protect its people from abuse, from famine, from genocide, then the outside world should be able to intervene as a last resort, with the use of force, if necessary. The Responsibility to Protect is an extraordinary doctrine. It is critical and controversial, and it is not just a product of the post–Cold War period or of media emphasis on these situations.

The common human desire to intervene on humanitarian grounds goes back a very long time. In ancient Rome, it was argued that human beings should be able to interfere to protect people at great risk, and in the nineteenth century the British fought slavery, against their own national interest. In

1820, the Romantic poet Lord Byron and the artist Eugène Delacroix fought against the Ottoman oppression of Greeks in the Greek War of Independence. So the desire to intervene on humanitarian grounds has existed for quite some time. It is a continual flame. Whether it can flicker beyond this point is part of our debate.

Let's start the debate with Gareth Evans.

GARETH EVANS: I hope that this debate begins and ends with a simple proposition. The proposition is this: whatever mistakes we make in the conduct of international relations, in responding to deadly conflict and human rights violations, let's not, as an international community, ever again fail to respond adequately to mass atrocities, to genocide, to ethnic cleansing, to other major crimes against humanity, and war crimes. Let's ensure that when another man-made humanitarian catastrophe like Cambodia or Rwanda or Bosnia or Darfur looms on the horizon, as it surely will, we, as an international community, will not have to look back at yet another disastrous failure. Let's get to the point where we won't ever again ask ourselves, with a mixture of anger and incomprehension and shame, how we could possibly have let this happen.

But how do we make that happen? Responsibility to end man-made humanitarian crises doesn't mean that for every problem of this kind the answer is to send in the marines. Collusive military force is a blunt and extreme instrument, and it should be used only in the most extreme and exceptional circumstances.

Professional soldiers usually agree, but civilians tend to be a little bit more gung-ho about the use of military force.

The trouble is that most of the debate on these issues is being conducted as if the use of extreme military force were the only option. Send in the marines or do nothing at all. There are, of course, cases where rapid and forceful coercive military intervention will be the only option. Roméo Dallaire was right about the need for military intervention in Rwanda in 1994. The Srebrenica massacre in Bosnia a year later was another case when the failure to react militarily was catastrophic. Kosovo in 1999 was another case where, although more controversial, military intervention was absolutely necessary in practice and thoroughly justified, if not legally, then morally.

But there are plenty of other cases where coercive military force — in the sense of mounting a full-scale military invasion as distinct from a consensual peacekeeping operation — is not the right answer, if only because to do so would cause considerably more harm than good.

We are deeply conscious of the unresolved crises in each of the particular countries that we're discussing in this debate — Sudan, Zimbabwe, Burma — and how much appalling human misery continues to be suffered by innocent civilians. We do have to rule out coercive military force as an option for reasons which we can debate later in detail.

That doesn't mean, however, that the alternative is to do nothing. There is a whole range of responses — from the supportive, to the persuasive, to the coercive. There is a toolbox of measures — diplomatic, economic, legal, and military — that can and should be used by the international community to prevent atrocities from occurring in the first place. These measures should be used to react to atrocities when they do occur, to rebuild societies that are shattered by crises, and to ensure the underlying causes are addressed so that these situations don't occur again.

This is the approach that is at the heart of the Responsibility to Protect doctrine. The international community endorsed R2P unanimously at the 2005 World Summit. Canada was instrumental in persuading the international community to embrace the doctrine. It is a more multi-layered and nuanced concept than the one-dimensional military-focused battle cry for humanitarian intervention. It is already apparent that this approach generates the kind of global reflex consensus response we need if we are going to respond effectively to these catastrophic, criminal situations.

Getting the public to appreciate the differences between the kinds of responses that are available is not going to be easy. Getting them to accept that ending humanitarian crises doesn't always mean using extreme and intrusive military force, and encouraging sensible discussion about other options, is not going to be easy either. I hope that during the course of this debate we'll be able to persuade you that there is a viable set of responses that don't involve military action.

My last word in opening this debate is to acknowledge that international engagement of any kind — whether it be extreme military action, or throwing resources at a problem, or trying to come to a solution through diplomatic mediation — is not cost-free for any government or for any of the individuals involved, particularly when it involves the willingness to spill blood for the cause in question.

So what is the justification for incurring that kind of cost?

Doesn't charity begin at home? Where is the national interest in mounting any of these international adventures, however noble the cause may be? Well, there is a national interest, and we want to talk about that national interest during this debate. It has a number of dimensions, but the critical one is this: in this day and age, the national interest is not something that can be pursued by the most expedient form of protection of immediate national security and economic interests. In this interdependent, globalized era, every country has a national interest in ensuring that atrocity crime situations in other countries are prevented or stopped. Even when they occur in faraway countries, it is in the national interest of everyone to prevent or stop them.

States that cannot or will not stop internal atrocity crimes are the kinds of states that cannot or will not stop terrorism, or weapons proliferation, or drug and people trafficking, or the spread of health pandemics, or other global risks which every country in the world wants to avoid. This debate is not just about national interests. It is about our common humanity.

There is a complex selection of tools at our disposal, and we should use them for reasons of national interest and we should do so for reasons of our common morality. If we don't respond to atrocity crime situations in this way, we simply won't be able to live with ourselves.

BRIAN STEWART: Thank you, Gareth. Ambassador Bolton, please. To be followed by Mia Farrow and then General Hillier.

JOHN BOLTON: Thank you very much. When advocates of the Responsibility to Protect talk, they talk in terms of the international community. I know where the international community lives. It's where I flew from yesterday, and it puts me in mind of the great American humorist Will Rogers, who once said, "I've been around so long I can remember way back when a liberal was someone who was generous with his own money and his own soldiers."

We're told that the use of military force with respect to humanitarian intervention is only a small part of the game. We're told that economic and diplomatic pressure can be applied as well. That's certainly true. But when it comes down to where the rubber meets the road, the point the humanitarian intervenors make is that it comes down to military force. And if you ignore that point, that's really saying nothing more than, "Do good, my children."

I won't argue against that sentiment. The point to consider is that R2P is not the same as UN peacekeeping. UN peacekeeping successes have occurred in the past because the parties involved in the dispute have consented to the UN's involvement. That is not the case in the Responsibility to Protect doctrine. UN peacekeeping is typically neutral between the parties of dispute. The point of the Responsibility to Protect is not to be neutral. And finally, UN peacekeeping operations have very limited rules of engagement. This is precisely the opposite of what humanitarian intervention implies.

Moreover, the rhetoric of humanitarian intervention is far broader than its advocates believe. This is one of the reasons why the debate over humanitarian intervention is not comprehensible at an abstract level.

Let's take, for example, the case of the citizens of North Korea, where over decades the height and weight of the average North Korean has declined. Despite this, no one considers humanitarian intervention in North Korea. What about a country where the government kills its political opponents, bans political parties, suppresses the press, and even goes so far as to threaten children with lower grades if their parents don't vote the right way? Am I talking about Zimbabwe? No, I'm talking about the last presidential election in Russia. Where is the Responsibility to Protect there? The fact is, these cases are too hard. So instead, the R2P focuses on those cases that are easy and cheap, or that people think will be easy and cheap.

The classic example was Somalia, which started off with an effort to open up channels of humanitarian aid distribution and ended with a failed exercise in nation-building. During the Battle of Mogadishu, eighteen American Rangers were dragged through the dusty streets of the city, and the situation in Somalia was worse after the intervention than before. Consider the consequences of the use of military force in Iraq and Afghanistan. Do you think it's easy, even for the U.S. military, the most powerful military in the history of the world, to avoid casualties to itself or to innocent civilians?

Consider those cases before casually advocating the use of military force even for high moral purposes. Then, ask yourself: who is responsible for making decisions on behalf of the international community? The advocates of Responsibility to Protect say it is the UN Security Council. The UN was unable to do anything during the great crises of the twentieth century and during the Cold War. It has also failed to respond adequately to international terrorism and the proliferation of weapons of mass destruction.

The UN has struggled for three years to put an effective peacekeeping force in Darfur, and has so far failed. This is a body that could barely bring itself to put Zimbabwe and Burma on its agenda, let alone try and reach some kind of substantive decision on those points. This is the body that you want to entrust to decide for the Responsibility to Protect? It is a frail reed, indeed.

I recognize that those who advocate for the Responsibility to Protect are well-intentioned. I respect those who believe in it as a doctrine, and I would simply say to all of you — and I say it to you with great respect: If you want to engage in humanitarian intervention, do it with your own sons and daughters, not with mine.

BRIAN STEWART: Mia Farrow, please.

MIA FARROW: If we were to debate whether or not we are obligated to act in the case of mass atrocities, then we are debating an obligation to which we are already committed. The Convention on the Prevention and Punishment of the Crime of Genocide of 1948 already obliges the countries that have signed it. In the case of genocide, the Genocide Convention of 1948 binds every party to it, and in the case of other major crimes against humanity, other treaties and conventions and declarations make up a body of international law that is clear and unequivocal.

The international community formed the United Nations

precisely because of such crimes. If the UN, or even the idea of an international community, is to mean anything, we must acknowledge our moral and legal obligations to act to protect civilians from mass atrocity crimes.

The most pragmatic reasons for early actions are irrefutable. It is far better and more effective to prevent such crimes than to respond after they have begun. We look first, of course, at the cost in human lives. But we must also consider the financial costs and the diplomatic complexity of trying to end a full-blown conflict. We should anticipate that unchecked mass atrocities will destabilize neighbouring countries, raising issues of international insecurity. We have only to look at Congo today to see the far-reaching, devastating effects of a crisis that began in Rwanda fourteen years ago.

We must also acknowledge that since interventions of one kind or another will inevitably occur, it is prudent to clarify and strengthen some established set of multilateral rules to limit the frequency of such interventions and to enhance their legitimacy.

The Genocide Convention, which was written sixty years ago, was clear and explicit. In 2005, this obligation was unanimously reaffirmed by the international community in the World Summit outcome document, which states that when states are manifestly failing to protect their population and should peaceful means be inadequate, we, as a community, must be prepared to take collective action. The member states have spoken. With the cumulative weight of these documents and the establishment of the International Criminal Court [ICC], a new concept of the international community is emerging. Sovereignty comes with responsibility. The World Summit outcome document was explicit on prevention. When early warning signs point to the fact that a nation is sliding toward a point where mass atrocity crimes are likely to occur, the UN, or its member states, need to dispatch the highest level envoys to negotiate a halt on such a slide. It is exclusively within the power of the UN Security Council to make sure that such envoys have at their disposal the full range of economic and diplomatic leverage, including sanctions and other penalties such as suspension of aid and trade, suspension of membership in international institutions, public criticism, arms embargo, a criminal investigation, and prosecution by the ICC. Detailed knowledge of a country could determine the sticks and the carrots.

You will note that I haven't mentioned military intervention. The core of this approach is preventative diplomacy — that is, de-escalating a situation before mass violence begins and before positions become entrenched. However, in my own view, it would be imprudent not to have a contingency plan. The idea that the United Nations might have a standing force to protect civilians from mass atrocity crimes and to allow humanitarian aid to reach those displaced by violence should be open for debate on its own merits. While people of good conscience hope and work tirelessly for the United Nations to become the peacekeeping, peace-building institution it was intended to be, the people of Darfur would remind us that we cannot rely solely on the UN.

As a community we must admit our best systems have

failed too often. As evidenced in Darfur, Burma, Somalia, and Congo, we have seen that if we take a clear and unflinching look at the UN, we see a painfully divided Security Council and the resultant paralysis. We have seen the tragic failures of the United Nations and its failure to protect the most vulnerable citizens on this planet.

For my own part, as a human being, I can only lend my voice to the chorus around the globe insisting that our leaders must do better. I believe our voices are insistent, and I believe that our moral determination can, if we are prepared to work tirelessly, produce the political resolve to shape a world in which all populations have the right to protection under the rule of law and to live without fear. We are standing at the threshold of a great evolution both in the United Nations and in the lifetime of humankind.

BRIAN STEWART: Thank you very much, Mia Farrow. Next, General Hillier.

RICK HILLIER: Our opponents have made some excellent points. The late, great baseball player Yogi Berra used to say, "In theory there is no difference between theory and practice. In practice there is." So that's what I'm going to talk to you about — the practice of intervention.

I realize that I'm the only one participating in this debate who has actually had the experience of being involved in intervention operations, and so I talk to you from the point of view of a soldier. And believe me, the responsibility falls to soldiers when diplomats and those who want to do good things — without question, for good reasons — scream that we must do something. That is always the answer — a vague "something." And we always believe that doing that "something" is going to be easy.

The diplomatic, legal, and financial pressures that we hear about and that should be applied usually don't work. If they did, we probably wouldn't have had to fight World War II, North Korea would be a democracy, and Osama bin Laden would be in jail somewhere as we speak. Remember, we are talking about armed men who operate from very base motives, and have used violence to win power, gain money, and remain immune from prosecution.

As a soldier, I saw that the international community had shown itself incapable of developing a strategy for any intervention efforts that it undertook. Tactics without strategy are akin to roads that are going nowhere and will lead to short-term focus on a mission. Let's face it, there is no strategy for Darfur. You can't have a strategy for Darfur, because then you must actually have one for Sudan, and you can't have a strategy for Sudan because you must have one for the region and the seven nations that border on Darfur. So, actually, what you're talking about is a grand strategy for the failed continent of Africa. Sadly, the international community hasn't shown the capacity or the capability to develop a strategy for Africa, let alone any of the other strategies that must therein be inclusive.

This lack of strategy results in incoherence in command and control, and it leads to short-term tactical benefits that disappear as soon as the troops depart. International cohesion is usually the first casualty of having tactics without a strategy to guide you.

In addition to this lack of strategy, there are institutions in the international community that are unfit for the present security environment. We have already been critical of the UN during this debate, but as one of my commanders once said, the United Nations is really about lessons observed from past intervention operations. In fact, a further comment of his was that the United Nations could not run a one-man rush to the latrine.

As for NATO, it is still very much focused on the Cold War. NATO simply does not work; its command structure reflects exactly that. With twenty-six to twenty-eight nations operating in consensus, making even minor tactical decisions is difficult. Where is the individual or the country that can actually put their lips on the blue lips of the decomposing corpse of those two organizations and breathe life back into them?

Further, the capacities and the capabilities necessary for intervention operations simply do not exist. In the military, special forces, intelligence, unmanned aerial vehicles [UAVs], and amphibious platforms are necessary for intervention operations, but they are simply not available. Of course, you also need soldiers, you need boots on the ground. If we were serious about participating in humanitarian interventions, the armed forces of Australia and Canada would have to be doubled in size. The civilian capabilities are simply not there.

Along with ensuring the security of a population in an intervention, you also have to help build a government, so that when you leave, you've left the country in an improved state. You have to develop the country in question, so that when you leave, the people there have hope for the future.

The capacity to go into a given country and do that sort of work does not exist in the international community.

Finally, the countries that comprise the international community simply do not have the collective will to conduct an enduring operation. We are conditioned by one-hour TV shows where you have a cataclysmic event followed by fifty minutes of events that sum it up before giving you a happy ending. We cannot expect the same results in an intervention operation. The reality is that all of those missions become enduring missions that go on for generations. Populations don't have the robustness of will to accept collateral damage, and that is dangerous because it leads to what we in the military call "TV tactics." This means shaping your tactics so that they appear better to the folks back home.

Let me conclude by saying that you might speak from the heart when you say we must do something, but the reality is that the international community and most of the countries that comprise the international community simply don't have the capabilities, the ability to develop strategy and institutions, and most importantly, the robustness of will for the kind of intervention operations we are talking about.

BRIAN STEWART: Thank you all for those tremendous opening statements. Let's examine some of them.

General Hillier, is it true the military is uneasy about intervention missions? They've had bad experiences in the past, but how much is it perhaps the resistance of generations of officers to developing a core intervention force, or to develop the required skills? How much might the military be acting as a sea anchor against international efforts to address intervention?

RICK HILLIER: I don't think that there is a core obstacle to intervention operations in most military forces. I think soldiers have realized that once we declare that we must do something, that declaration turns into some action or idea that quickly deteriorates and becomes a responsibility left to the soldier. So you have the soldiers carrying the weight of the mission, and they have precious little support. I should say that though I'm wearing a suit and not a uniform, I'm here as a soldier. And as soldiers we know that we're going to do our job. We're trained, structured, equipped, and prepared to do our job one small mission at a time. What we do worry about is that we don't have the capacity to take that small operation and turn it into a long-term stable structure that will last after we leave. Those capabilities, and the public will, are not there.

Where is, for example, "government in a box"[1]? Which organization in our world, in our country, in any country actually, has a deployable government-building battalion designed to do what was done in World War II? I'm not talking about individuals. I'm talking about a trained, built, cohesive military that you deploy into Darfur, into Afghanistan, in order to help build the kind of government they need to sustain their country after we leave.

GARETH EVANS: Are you saying there is no capability in the entire international community to provide the 5,000 troops

---

[1] The term "government in a box" refers to General Stanley A. McChrystal's plan for the Marja campaign in Afghanistan.

that your colleague Roméo Dallaire advocated for so per-
suasively and that would have made a difference to 800,000
lives in Rwanda in 1994? Are you saying there's no capability right now in an international community that has a
military inventory of 11,842 helicopter units at last count,
but has been unable collectively to supply twenty-two of
them to the peacekeeping operations in Darfur, knowing
they would make one hell of a difference to the effectiveness
of the human protection operation on the ground? There
may be a lack of political will, I don't disagree with that, but
capability? Come on, this is a straw man.

RICK HILLIER: There is a problem with strategy, there is a
problem with the robustness of will, and there is a problem
if you have capability but simply don't have the will to use it.
So yes, there may be some helicopters available, but they are
useless if they're not in Afghanistan or Darfur. It's virtually
the same thing as not having the capability.

Even in missions for which countries have signed up you
still cannot find the troops, the helicopters, or the equipment
to do the job on the ground. Yet hundreds of billions of dollars are being spent on other things which are not related to
humanitarian intervention.

BRIAN STEWART: Does not intervention occasionally work?
Remember the British marines, the Royal Navy going into
Sierra Leone to back up UN troops in 2000, or French forces
going into Côte D'Ivoire in 2003? Haven't there been times
when troops from Britain or France have been able to move
quickly and put a lid on the violence?

MIA FARROW: Right now a European Union force is deployed effectively on the Darfur/Chad border.

RICK HILLIER: I would say the jury is still out on the effectiveness of the EU force deployed on the Darfur/Chad border. It is a temporary calm in one area, but will it last? The question is, will it achieve anything greater than a temporary calm, and can it be maintained long enough to get some good out of it? What I would say about Sierra Leone and the Ivory Coast is that one nation leading, not an international community effort per se, is the key. And, as in Darfur, you have to ask, is that change actually going to hold? We all hope it does but it's certainly not guaranteed, and the fact is there was already a structure or participants in place in those areas that wanted to see the conflict resolved. That doesn't exist in Sudan, where the government itself doesn't want to resolve the issue.

BRIAN STEWART: John Bolton, you raised a very interesting ethical question in your presentation that some might find a slippery argument. And that is that we, the world, have not put sufficient pressure on the giants, China or Russia, when they abuse human rights and when they go even further into state-sanctioned murder. So the dilemma is whether we ought to take on the small powers if we can't take on the big ones.

JOHN BOLTON: No, I don't think that's the argument at all. Even the advocates of Responsibility to Protect don't seriously believe that they can do anything about North Korea, which is a large prison camp, or Russia, or a number of other examples I could cite. This is an acknowledgement of a critical point, which is that any intervention has to be considered on its own merits, and the cost and benefits have to be weighed on their own merits. That's why in the abstract, in my view, this discussion is essentially meaningless.

GARETH EVANS: We've had more straw men erected here tonight than in seventeen showings of *The Wizard of Oz*. I mean, there was Rick's little excursion at the beginning, and then we've had John Bolton saying the Responsibility to Protect is only about military intervention, and if you can't engage in military intervention in some of these cases, then the whole doctrine, the whole concept, is meaningless. We've also heard that if we can't deal with human rights violations of the kind that are occurring in countries like Russia and elsewhere, then the concept is again meaningless.

But the point is that the Responsibility to Protect is only about a very small subset of the conflicts and human rights violations that are occurring in the world. It's only when mass atrocity crimes are occurring or are anticipated that we invoke the Responsibility to Protect, and in those situations the repertoire of available responses is vast and extends across the whole range of diplomatic and economic pressure, legal prosecution before the International Criminal Court, and much else.

JOHN BOLTON: I'm going to read two sentences, only two sentences, of the outcome document from the 2005 World Summit on this subject. Paragraph 139 states: "The international community, through the United Nations, also has the responsibility to use appropriate diplomatic, humanitarian and other peaceful means, in accordance with Chapters VI and VIII of the Charter [of the United Nations], to help to protect populations from genocide, war crimes, ethnic cleansing and crimes against humanity. In this context, we are prepared to take collective action, in a timely and decisive manner, through the Security Council, in accordance with the Charter, including Chapter VII, on a case-by-case basis and in co-operation with relevant regional organizations as appropriate, should peaceful means be inadequate and national authorities are manifestly failing to protect their populations from genocide, war crimes, ethnic cleansing and crimes against humanity." Now that's clear, isn't it?

GARETH EVANS: This is the way you conducted yourself at the United Nations. You arrived with 400 amendments in your bag and you destroyed single-handedly the potential for consensus on a mess of other issues. You didn't succeed.

JOHN BOLTON: If you want to argue the merits, then let's argue the merits. But let's stop the personal attacks.

GARETH EVANS: You did not succeed in destroying consensus on the Responsibility to Protect paragraphs in the World outcome document because they were remarkably clear. The paragraphs say three things: (1) that sovereign countries have the responsibility not to perpetrate atrocity crimes against their own people; (2) that other countries have the responsibility to assist them in creating the capacity to ensure that they will act that way if they are willing to do so; and (3) that where states manifestly fail to exercise that responsibility, then it's the responsibility of the wider international community to step in under Chapter VII of the Charter.

BRIAN STEWART: I'd like to change the direction slightly. Mia Farrow, a very serious objection was raised here, by both Rick Hillier and John Bolton, and that is that when countries decide to intervene, they are risking the lives of their own soldiers. And while the public may sympathize with these interventions at first, people often begin to question whether or not the intervention is in the national interest. Why is an intervention in a very faraway place like Darfur or Rwanda or the Congo in the national interest?

MIA FARROW: Let's not leap to the conclusion that an intervention means a military intervention, because there are myriad options before we arrive at that point. A military intervention would only be utilized if what I referred to as "sticks and carrots" failed. I have pages of things that an envoy can do. We saw the success of that just now — former Secretary General of the UN Kofi Annan travelled to Kenya to participate in negotiations to end the civil unrest there as the country was sliding toward something very ugly indeed. Kofi Annan was able to negotiate an agreement, and there was a cessation of violence in Kenya. So we've seen diplomatic intervention at work. Intervention doesn't necessarily mean military intervention.

Forgive me, with all due respect, General Hillier, but

your insistence that any action must be a military invasion is a deeply flawed argument. You've ignored the nature of the African Union/United Nations Hybrid operation [UNAMID] in Darfur and its goals, and the nature of the negotiations between the United Nations and Khartoum. Those negotiations did result in United Nations Resolution 1769, which did result in a peacekeeping force that is there — albeit compromised — and I've spoken to military, private military, and U.S. military generals, and the troops there are sufficient in number. But they are under-supported and undertrained. Were they fully supported by the international community — and there are stipulations about African countries that the force must be African in character in African countries — they would be fully able, at 9,000, to do the job.

RICK HILLIER: If diplomatic, financial, and legal measures and the rule of law were significant enabling levers, we wouldn't be having this debate. It comes down to the fact that the vast majority of interventions occur because those measures simply don't work. There may be the rare case when these measures are effective in a preventative manner. But more often than not it comes down to putting young men and women on the ground. And when you put them on the ground in compromised missions, you are putting their lives at risk without moral high ground, without being able to explain to them why. The military forces are not going to be able to assist the people on the ground the way they need to be assisted, and further, you're not going to leave a sustainable structure behind that's going to make life better for the citizens of the country. You're probably going to make it worse.

BRIAN STEWART: But could one make the argument that one of the reasons diplomatic efforts fail is due to the generals who are saying, "We don't want to intervene"? So there's no looming threat of military intervention?

JOHN BOLTON: The three states in Darfur are geographically the size of France. The distances are large, and there is no infrastructure. It is precisely because the African Union peacekeeping mission failed that people said we need an outside force; and yet in repeated negotiations over Security Council resolutions, the government of Sudan, supported by China, objected to the kind of UN force that many were calling for. Why is the government supported by China? Because China has large and growing energy needs, and it wants the oil and natural gas assets that are controlled by the government in Khartoum. So why is there a requirement that there be a joint command between the African Union and the UN? Joint command is a prescription for real trouble down the road, as was the case in Somalia. And why is there a requirement that the forces be predominantly African? Because the government of Sudan and its friends on the Security Council have consistently watered down efforts to have an effective UN peacekeeping force. This is the reality of the Security Council, and this is the reality of military action in Sudan.

MIA FARROW: He's right about the division in the Security

Council and China. China has been propping up all of these regimes — Zimbabwe, Burma, Sudan. China on the Security Council has been a major problem.

BRIAN STEWART: But have you not been working at ways to shame China into action?

MIA FARROW: I was surprised that I could write an op-ed that prompted China into action. That op-ed was published in the *Wall Street Journal,* and an article about that article appeared on the front page of the *New York Times* a week later because it prompted China to act.

BRIAN STEWART: We did somehow slip over the point that I was trying to get at. The point is that eventually, in many of these cases, military force might be used. The question then becomes: what democracy is willing to risk the lives of their sons and daughters in a foreign war for a cause that is not in that country's national interest?

GARETH EVANS: The truth of the matter is that there is a national interest which is universally acknowledged: ensuring that fragile and failing states don't descend into catastrophe, because if they do they put the rest of us at risk.

We saw that, of course, with Afghanistan harbouring the Taliban. We've seen it potentially applicable to Somalia, with the harbouring of terrorists and the transit of weapons of mass destruction. Certainly, we've seen the potential and the reality in many of these cases around the world with the spread of refugee camps, health pandemics, drug and people trafficking, and all the things that impact upon us.

I think we have to take these considerations into account in making the calculation of what is in the national interest, as well as take into account the moral interest that is unquestionably involved here and the public sentiment, which is clear every time you're tested on these issues. If the public can see the nature of the horror that's unfolding as well as a rational relationship between a commitment of this kind and a positive result, they'll support it. And that's because people are basically decent.

JOHN BOLTON: Morality is important to all of us. But in many conflicts morality doesn't come conveniently divided into two distinct sides. This is certainly true in Darfur, where the government in Khartoum has unquestionably been committing the bulk of the gross abuses of human rights and committing genocide, as U.S. Secretary of State Colin Powell said, but the rebels are hardly free from blame, nor are they a cohesive force.

When you say that national interest encompasses this broad abstraction, you've made national interest into an impossible distraction as well. America saw this concretely in Somalia in 1993 during the Battle of Mogadishu. Any American president has to make a wrenching decision when he puts young Americans in harm's way, and morality doesn't all come down on one side in that calculation either.

MIA FARROW: Had we intervened in Darfur in some capacity in 2003 and 2004, it would have been a far more simple scenario, it would have been far more easily resolved before the rebel groups splintered. We did have a very clear bad, bad guy in that scenario.

JOHN BOLTON: I must say, I'm reminded of members of the Bush administration advocating the invasion of Iraq. They also said how simple it would be.

MIA FARROW: That situation was a fiasco.

GARETH EVANS: Which side do you want on that debate, John?

JOHN BOLTON: I was in favour of the invasion. You see, this is an argument that essentially says the use of military force is best only when there's no national interest at stake, and when you think there is national interest at stake you shouldn't use military force.

RICK HILLIER: We see national interest articulated differently every single day by different people, who sometimes confuse those interests with values. And when that confusion takes place, the support that Gareth speaks of, the support of a population who see bad things being done and want to march to the sound of the guns and actually do something about it, that support starts to disappear quickly. Especially when (a) coverage of the situation disappears from TV screens and (b) the first bodies of those young men and women start coming back home. When a young soldier is on those dirty, dusty, dangerous trails, that nation must walk with him or her if they're going to be successful in doing what we ask them to do.

MIA FARROW: But when it comes to protecting an unarmed civilian population, I can't believe I'm alone in that I would volunteer my children. I'm not talking about overthrowing a government or shooting every kid on a camel, I'm talking about defending defenseless civilian populations.

RICK HILLIER: And what I would say to you is this: you would fail because you're approaching from the heart. What I'm saying is that a ruthless, pragmatic approach by the international community would be better. And the international community needs the United Nations resuscitated. If President-elect Barack Obama can resuscitate that organization and give it some capability, and when we have countries signed up beforehand with the proper nation-building tools, then we might have a vision for what we're doing, and a strategy. So far, the international community appears incapable of being able to do those things.

But I want to go back to the point about the generals at home not wanting to intervene, which Brian laid out a few moments ago. I think the generals, the ones that I know, from many nations, are very pragmatic and very loyal men and women. They want to do what's right, and they want to take on the operations that are in our national interests and in the interests of a stable world. But they also know that the burden will follow them, and the other members of the international community will not help because the capabilities are not yet there.

BRIAN STEWART: I want to say one thing. We have this image of your average soldier going to a country you may not have heard of, dying, and then people asking why his or her life was wasted on a foreign cause. Every Western military has big, glamorous special forces, quickly trained to go anywhere, especially to areas where new conflict has broken out. We could replay the events that happened on the ground in Rwanda and probably 1,000 soldiers could have put down that massacre of 800,000. We seem to have ever more spectacular military resources. But is it not the unwillingness of politicians and generals to risk casualties that prevents some interventions?

RICK HILLIER: Not at all. First of all, I question whether a 1,000- or 5,000-strong force could make a difference, or would have made a difference in Rwanda. When we reformed our military structure that brought us smaller units and more sophisticated military technology, we thought we wouldn't need as many troops. What we have discovered in operations since 2001 is that God remains on the side of big battalions, and we need boots on the ground and we need many soldiers to have an effect in helping secure populations. I don't think 1,000 troops in Rwanda would have made a single bit of difference, nor would have 5,000 troops. It would have required a lot of men and women on the ground. Should we have been there? In all truth, absolutely. But with a hell of a lot more than 5,000 troops.

BRIAN STEWART: You were one of the first, General Hillier, to go into Afghanistan and make the statement that, yes, people really warmed to the idea of Canada helping the Afghan people towards a better life, towards education for their children, but Canada went in to protect its own national security interests. We were part of an international obligation to make sure that the Taliban didn't again allow a safe haven for al Qaeda. It seemed to morph into the kind of humanitarian intervention mission now that you doubt could work elsewhere.

RICK HILLIER: Of course, you realize that we went into Afghanistan as a nation long before I became the Chief of the Defence Staff.

There are those who say that we went into Afghanistan because we did not want to go to Iraq, and that's why our troops initially showed up on the ground in Afghanistan. Yes, Canada has honourable goals. Yes, we believe that our national interests are at stake in that region. But all of the things that I have discussed during this debate are things that I've lived through both as a commander inside Afghanistan, and then as the Chief of Defence Staff. I made those decisions once the government had given me the direction to send our young men and women there.

BRIAN STEWART: But my point here is that when you go to the military and ask, why we are in Afghanistan until the end of 2011, they don't say that it's to stop the Taliban taking over and Afghanistan becoming a rogue state. They say, well, the Afghan people need security, they need a better life, they need agriculture, more education. It's becoming more of a back-door humanitarian mission.

GARETH EVANS: Brian, I think that statement misrepresents

the situation because what we set out to do, as an international community, in Afghanistan, was an exercise in self-defence after the Taliban attack on the United States. We're still trying to rebuild that failed state in order to ensure that there's no resumption of a Taliban-led government of the kind that will create similar problems for us in the future. In order to complete that rebuilding operation as an international community, we have to address issues surrounding confidence in government, and issues of fairness with which everybody is now wrestling.

But this is a long way from fire brigade operations used in extreme cases when all else has failed to stop immediate mass atrocity crimes, and genocide of the kind that we saw in Rwanda. Military operations are always ugly, always horrible, always bloody, always awful for those who lose their kids or their relatives. But sometimes in extreme cases we have to do it.

BRIAN STEWART: I understand your objection. But what I'm describing is how the mission in Afghanistan is justified to the Canadian people now, and that is the way it tends to be justified. Mia Farrow, does hearing these views make you more pessimistic?

MIA FARROW: No, I've heard much worse than this. I'm absolutely convinced that we can summon the political will, and that the discussion has to start at the grassroots level in rooms such as this one. So I go from place to place and appeal to governments, I've been before the U.S. Congress three times, and before the Senate three times. I go from campus to campus, divestment hearing to divestment hearing, and I think in the United States, anyway, we're seeing the largest response to an African atrocity, Darfur, since apartheid. So I do think we can summon the political will, and we must if we are to have a world that's worth giving to our children. And if we're all to sit here and say, well, that's it, this was the best we could do and everything else is impossible, then we might as well call an end to it and take the cyanide and drink the hemlock. I think that if we don't have the will, then we should get out of the kitchen and leave the cooking to someone who does have the will and does have the stomach for it.

BRIAN STEWART: Mr. Bolton, what about the argument that maybe things aren't changing and that certain countries might take a new look at United Nations reform? Your experience has been negative, but do you rule out the possibility that the Responsibility to Protect might be worked into applicable international doctrine?

JOHN BOLTON: No. I think you have to be practical about the Security Council. We tried to put Burma on the Security Council agenda as a threat to international peace and security for a variety of reasons. The Chinese objected over and over again. We finally forced it to a vote on whether the Security Council would discuss Burma, and we won that vote. China voted no because it was a procedural vote. China didn't have veto power, but there's no doubt — and there hasn't been since the day we won the procedural vote — that if we tried to do anything in the Security Council with any meaningful impact on Burma, that China would veto it.

So I think the question for the advocates who say that we've got to do something and use more than military force is, what happens when the Security Council won't act?

GARETH EVANS: Can I introduce a slightly more optimistic note about what has been achieved by the much-maligned UN and Security Council over the years since the end of the Cold War? A Canadian institution, Simon Fraser University, has gathered stats on this, and they are compelling. The reality is that there has been an 80 percent decline in the number of serious conflicts with 1,000 or more casualties of war a year over the last eighteen years. There has also been a decline of that magnitude in the number of mass atrocity crimes of the kind we've addressed during this debate. Why? The analysis suggests that there has been a remarkable increase in international commitment, mainly through the United Nations, but also through some regional organizations, to effect diplomatic peacemaking operations with expanded mandates of human protection now enacted regularly by the Security Council. There has also been a much expanded commitment to post-conflict peacekeeping to ensure that there's no relapse into these atrocity situations.

All of that is good news, and I think we ought to recognize it because it does mean that our efforts are not wasted. And most of those strategies have not involved the aggressive use of invasive coercive military force.

BRIAN STEWART: General Hillier, do you think Afghanistan is going to be a concern for Canada for three more years? Do you think, after Canada withdraws, the Canadian military and the Canadian public will be ready to return to peace-keeping in more operations abroad and developing some of the trends Gareth Evans mentioned?

RICK HILLIER: I think that the Canadian military certainly would be ready to recover, to prepare for other missions abroad, or to participate in missions closer to Canada, and to do so at the direction of the government. But are we leaving behind things that might actually work, such as government institutions and economic systems? Where is the battalion that's going to go and train a police force in Darfur or in Zimbabwe or in Burma once we have helped them build a government and actually changed their political structure?

BRIAN STEWART: But that's something the Canadian government could aim to develop in the future.

RICK HILLIER: The point is that those initiatives have to be started and developed correctly. Right now, the capabilities to do to achieve these goals — such as leaving an effective police force — are minuscule at best. I'm worried that we'll go in and do the security piece, train an army well, and then allow a corrupt, inept government to take power.

BRIAN STEWART: One thing I'm really curious about is whether there's any indication that the tyrants of the world are becoming more uncomfortable, that they feel heat on their back? Even with international courts and international pressure, is there any evidence that tyrants are sitting in their presidential palaces a little more nervous about committing atrocities and brutalities?

GARETH EVANS: The response to the indictment of Sudanese President Omar Hassan Ahmad al-Bashir at the International Criminal Court is a much more careful response than was being feared by a number of commentators, who said the prosecution was going to set the place alight. I believe the ICC is altering behaviour. The international criminal process has been the most important single form of pressure introduced into international affairs in recent times. It's just a pity that the United States opposed it for so long, and I hope that under the new administration we'll have a full-throated commitment to the international criminal process.

RICK HILLIER: I'd like to make a comment on that topic. I don't think the President of Sudan's behaviour is changing. The lead story on the BBC this afternoon was the fact that he is selling all the fertile land along the Nile River to other countries in Africa and the Middle East so they can grow crops to feed their populations while a good part of his country's population starves. So I'm not sure the effect really has taken hold in Sudan as you describe.

GARETH EVANS: So what is your solution for Sudan, for Darfur at the moment? What kind of leverage would you apply?

RICK HILLIER: The first thing I would say is that diplomatic incentives are not working, and financial incentives are not working or are not sufficient. What you have to do is look at how rich President al-Bashir is, and how rich the group of men and/or women who actually run the country are, and see what you can do to force them to behave better.

The legal constraints on killing people are clearly not working, either. So it would require a strategy for Africa, as opposed to a strategy for Darfur, which simply won't work.

JOHN BOLTON: I'd like to answer your question on whether there is an effect on leaders around the world. I have to say I think the evidence goes in the other direction. The Kremlin recently ordered military forces to cross an international border into the territory of a state, a former state of the Soviet Union, for the first time since the breakup of the Soviet Union in 1991. And they used the argument that they had to protect ethnic Russians in South Ossetia from Georgian interference.

The Russian government is handing out Russian passports to ethnic Russians in the Ukraine, obviously laying the basis for a subsequent argument that they're going to protect the Russians in the Ukraine. If you look at the use of aggressive military force by a nuclear armed power, you can see it before us in the past few months. We are approaching a very tense situation in the subcontinent between India and Pakistan due to the terrorist attacks conducted against vital Indian interests.

Let me close with another example. We are seeing international piracy, based in Somalia, of a magnitude we haven't seen since the nineteenth century. And NATO has been unable to do anything about it for fear — among other things — of being prosecuted for violating the human rights of the pirates.

BRIAN STEWART: I think it's time to bring the audience in now. One audience member asks: "What should be the determining factor in deciding whether to intervene — national interests or national values?" Mia Farrow, why don't I start with you on that?

MIA FARROW: Actually, Gareth has listed these so magnificently in his book, *The Responsibility to Protect*, which I highly recommend. So perhaps you ought to leave that one to Gareth.

BRIAN STEWART: National interests or national values?

GARETH EVANS: It's a combination of both, because national interest does extend in the way that I previously described. National interest also exists in reputational form. Every country has a national interest in being perceived as a good international citizen — an area where Canada has led the world traditionally. In pursuing these issues beyond ourselves, a country can benefit from the respect that flows from other countries when they demonstrate a willingness to put treasure and sometimes even blood into advancing these particular cases, so national interests and values do, in a way, overlap.

If you mean militarily, there's a lot of criteria to satisfy before you even get to that. You have to satisfy the threshold criteria and the seriousness of the harm to the people who are victims of atrocity. You have to satisfy criteria of last resort, of proportionality, of right intention, and above all, the balance of consequences. You have to be confident that you are actually going to do more good than harm. There are very few cases where, when you apply those criteria, you can justify coercive military invasion and even give rise to this judgement about national interest. There are a lot of hurdles to jump over and rightly so, because war is an ugly business.

RICK HILLIER: You cannot separate national interests completely from some national values. But you have to have a method of approach, a strategy, and you have to have a set of conditions to have a chance of success.

JOHN BOLTON: In his autobiography, Colin Powell told a story which took place in the early days of U.S. President Bill Clinton's administration when they were debating what action to take in Somalia. U.S. Ambassador to the UN Madeleine Albright said to General Powell, "What's the point of having this wonderful military if you're not prepared to use it?" Powell said that he just about had an aneurysm as a result of that kind of attitude. And I agree; I think we have to guard against that attitude.

BRIAN STEWART: One question for the entire panel: How are humanitarian interventions different from past attempts by Western powers to civilize developing nations?

GARETH EVANS: Leaders in the developing world are suspicious;

they believe that this talk of humanitarian intervention is an excuse for the big guys to throw their weight around — more of the civilizing missions that developing nations experienced so often in the past. And when you have many countries who are very conscious of their fragility and coming into the international system, they're going to be very resistant to signing on to any generalized doctrine or intervention of that kind.

That's why there was so much debate and disagreement about intervention in the 1990s. There was a gulf between developing countries and the Western world — the Western world that was all too enthusiastic about intervention. The whole point of developing the Responsibility to Protect concept was to bridge the gulf between those two extreme positions.

MIA FARROW: The first option is to work with the nation in question, helping it to use its own capabilities to bring about its own resolutions.

RICK HILLIER: And I would agree with that. One of the first things that should be done is to reinforce the country's existing government structure and to help the government become effective and efficient enough that they can deliver what the population needs. I think there is a significant difference between what we are discussing now and past interventions with a so-called mission of civilizing the population. The civilization of the population of Africa resulted in the deaths of millions of proxy soldiers in the First World War, slavery, endemic diseases that spread throughout the continent, and a variety of other ills. I'm not sure that African nations can withstand more humanitarian interventions of that nature.

Right now, global communication changes everything. Events in Darfur, Afghanistan, Zimbabwe, or Burma, or anywhere else, are seen and heard instantly. That changes things dramatically.

I would also say that the stateless threats that we see out there are different now. Yes, we had that kind of thing in the past, but extremist groups, terrorist groups, criminal groups linked by global communications and with the ability to travel back and forth instantly now – well, I think the dynamic of an intervention has changed. That's why I reiterate that you have to have a strategy, not only Darfur or Sudan, not even for the seven or eight countries around it. But you've got to have a strategy to look after the ailing continent of Africa as a whole.

MIA FARROW: I resent [your] referring to the continent of Africa as a failed continent. We're looking at very separate nations with very separate goals, cultures, and languages which have to be respected, each on their own terms. I'm not talking about the colonial divisions, but all that Africa is. And yes, there are success stories in Africa, and yes, there are failures in Africa. Failures and a collapsed state in Africa, or anywhere else, serves no one, and is in no one's national interest.

We've seen evidence of that when we talk about pirates off the coast of Somalia. Pirates are off the coast of Somalia because it is a collapsed state. If Darfur were a separate nation it would be a collapsed state. We see how the situation in Darfur is destabilizing Chad, we see its effect on the Central African Republic, and I go back to the African Union force. Let's not too readily dismiss them, because wherever those troops are deployed — and I've seen it firsthand — those people feel safe, those women are able to go out and collect firewood. The basic right of a human being to wake up in the morning and not live in terror. That was the benefit provided by the African Union force.

I'll be sorry when that force leaves, and everyone along that border land will be, as well. I think you have to credit them with some measure of success. They're altruistic, they're not looking for regime change. They are simply protecting a civilian population, the people in camps, and the humanitarian workers trying to sustain them.

RICK HILLIER: We need a strategy for Darfur that encompasses all of its neighbouring countries, which equates roughly to the northern part of Africa. I would be happy to see a strategy for the Congo and Zimbabwe and all of their neighbours, which encompasses essentially the southern part of Africa as opposed to the failed continent of Africa, as I stated. That was the wrong way to put it.

JOHN BOLTON: Based on my experience dealing with African ambassadors at the UN headquarters in New York, and from private conversations, there is no group more acutely aware of the failings of the United Nations and its inability to deliver aid to Africa than the Africans themselves. Once they break loose from the stifling political correctness, you'd be surprised to hear what they have to say about the UN, but not publicly.

MIA FARROW: What would you propose instead? We all agree the United Nations needs to be improved. What are you proposing to do about that?

JOHN BOLTON: It's not my obligation. The Responsibility to Protect specifically says it's the Security Council that decides when the intervention will take place, agreed? That's what it says, which is where we are in Darfur.

GARETH EVANS: But nobody is arguing that Darfur is the place for military intervention.

JOHN BOLTON: We are talking about military intervention in Darfur and the deployment of a UN peacekeeping force. The argument is about replacing the failed inadequate African Union force with a more robust force. Kofi Annan once proposed NATO-equipped troops with greater logistical capability and more helicopter transport to overcome the lack of infrastructure. That's what Kofi Annan wanted, and that's what has been prevented from taking place in the Security Council. So you can talk about aspirations all you want, but until you explain how we get through the problem of the Security Council, you're just spinning wheels.

GARETH EVANS: Let's clarify that there is a huge difference between a voluntary consensual peacekeeping force of the kind that has now been approved in full by the Security Council and

sending in an invasion force. We're sure the Sudanese government is being obstructive, but individual states, including the
Western states, are unable or unwilling to supply this peacekeeping force with the resources — including helicopters —
that it needs.

There's a difference between that set of problems and
a humanitarian intervention in the traditional sense, and
you're just running the two things together. Nobody is arguing for an invasion force in Darfur, because to do so would be
wholly unproductive for the survival of the two and a half
million refugees there.

MIA FARROW: The protection of civilians and humanitarians
is a different issue. We're not talking about Iraq. We're talking about going in to protect civilians and humanitarians.

JOHN BOLTON: What I was trying to say was — and this is
the point I made at the beginning — that I think it's especially important to understand that humanitarian intervention is very different from traditional UN peacekeeping.
In the case of Darfur, Sudan and its allies on the Security
Council have, for more than three years, prevented the
deployment of the peacekeeping force. It is still not clear
when that will actually happen on the ground in Darfur, as
opposed to the halls of the United Nations. In the mean-
time the tragedy goes on. If you fault the governments
of the West for not contributing troops, how do you get
past the African Union, which doesn't want Western forces
occupying the region?

GARETH EVANS: They want helicopters, John, and they're not going to get them.

JOHN BOLTON: Well, it is fine to complain about inaction, but at some point you have to say that the inaction reflects the unwillingness of governments to do what people are calling for. This is what Rick Hillier was saying before. If you're not attuned to the reality you can propose remedies that won't happen, and while you're proposing them the situation will deteriorate even more.

MIA FARROW: Who was in government? You, sir. So, yes, I think when you're talking about the failure of governments you're talking about the failure of my government and your government.

JOHN BOLTON: Actually, three of us have been in government at different points, but I want to tell you I wish you could have been with the U.S. mission in New York when we were arguing to put Burma on the agenda of the Security Council. I wish you could have sat with us during those negotiations — not in the public chamber of the Security Council that we see on television, but in the informal meeting chamber arguing with China and other countries about why they didn't want us to talk about Burma.

GARETH EVANS: I agree. It's a travesty, you're right.

BRIAN STEWART: Big power politics and the ability of the superpowers to use leverage and get things done is part of the reality of the world. I still don't quite understand why, on the Security Council, there has not been a concerted effort to embarrass China and embarrass Russia if necessary. The Olympic Games proved very useful when it came to embarrassing China.

JOHN BOLTON: May I just give you one example? One of the overwhelming cultural attributes of the Security Council is the desire for unanimity. Most countries — including Britain, France, almost all of the members of the European Union that serve on the Council, and the majority of Third World countries — argue that it's more important to have a unanimous Security Council resolution than a more effective resolution that has a couple of negative votes. I think that it is wrong. I think it's in fact a good thing to make countries stand out in the rain from time to time.

The U.S. has to stand out in the rain occasionally when members of the Security Council veto resolutions that are unfair to Israel. It doesn't bother me to do that, nor should it bother governments on the Security Council to say we're not going to compromise this resolution any further, let's go to a vote. And if China wants to stand out and veto it, fine. Let China face the consequences.

My view is in a distinct minority. But if you think that consensus decision-making on the Security Council is so important that it should override these other concerns, then you have to acknowledge that you're not going to have resolutions that are as effective or as positive as you might otherwise have.

RICK HILLIER: This conversation confirms everything that scared me when I was on a mission working for the United Nations and I was trying to interpret the mumbo-jumbo that came from UN headquarters.

BRIAN STEWART: I have a question from the audience here addressed to Gareth Evans: "Was Russia's use of the humanitarian rationale for invading Georgia precipitated? Was it a result of NATO's humanitarian intervention in Kosovo?"

GARETH EVANS: Russia's attempt to explain its actions in Georgia in terms of the Responsibility to Protect was a travesty of the first order. Defending their own citizens when they created those citizens by issuing Russian passports for them, then going into Georgia with the use of military force when the provocation was probably there, but certainly not such as to justify military intervention. It certainly wasn't a last resort, just as the United States and Britain's use of the concept of humanitarian intervention or Responsibility to Protect was utterly misguided in the context of Iraq in 2003.

I have no doubt that Russia felt itself slightly justified in doing what it did in Georgia because of the events that took place in Kosovo. But frankly, there was no contest in terms of the nature of those two exercises. Kosovo in 1999 was a situation of massive ethnic cleansing, and given all that President Slobodan Milošević had done previously, there was every reason to believe it was going to be followed by genocide. It was a totally justified case for international military intervention.

The Security Council didn't endorse military intervention, so the coalition took action with NATO without the endorsement of the Security Council. That made it a very tough call for those of us wrestling with the rectitude of this response. The only answer you could possibly give was it was not legally right for the U.S. and other nations to do what they did, but it was certainly morally justified. It's the international equivalent to mitigation in domestic law.

Yes, we broke the law, but we were justified in doing so. You can do that occasionally, but you can't do it all the time.

JOHN BOLTON: I'm glad that point came up, because it shows that you can ignore the Security Council in some cases when it happens to be convenient for you, and yet attack other nations when their positions are inconvenient.

GARETH EVANS: It just happened to be convenient for a few hundred thousand Kosovo citizens who weren't killed, but I really do think that's a debating point that ought to be avoided.

RICK HILLIER: That's simplifying the issue also, though, because tens of thousands of Kosovo Serbian citizens in the northern part of the province now feel themselves under massive threat and feel their homes and their lives are going to be destroyed, or have been destroyed, by those same implications from the intervention itself. So it is not always cut and dried, and, yes, maybe some lives were saved. But the long-term implications still have not been felt in the southern part of Eastern Europe.

BRIAN STEWART: We're moving toward the end of the debate, but first we have closing statements. I will ask John Bolton to speak first, followed by Mia Farrow, Rick Hillier, and Gareth Evans. Three minutes each, please.

JOHN BOLTON: We've discussed morality a lot during this debate, and obviously all of us view moral questions as the most important we face as individuals. They should be, but I think it's very important to understand that morality does not always point in one direction. There can be legitimate disagreements among conflicting moral principles. You may not agree with the operational conclusions that follow from one set of moral arguments, but that doesn't mean that you're ignoring the moral question or that you're prepared to act immorally.

The highest morality that an American president has is the protection of American life. He is elected under our Constitution to lead the nation, to be the Commander-in-Chief, and to defend American interests and values around the world. Every American president thinks long and hard before deploying American forces into harm's way, and it should not be an object of denigration when an American president says, "In my judgement, as horrible as the situation across the sea may be, my moral imperatives lead me to conclude that American troops should not be deployed into that situation."

That's not immoral. That's a disagreement about moral principles, and when the disagreement can be played out in the loss of life of young men and women, it is serious indeed. So when you think about this question, I simply urge you to not be casual with other people's blood.

MIA FARROW: On a personal note, some of you may know that I am a mother of fourteen children. My children and I are not, for the most part, related by blood, but by something much stronger, by love and the deepest kind of commitment. My children come to me from all the corners of the earth. We are a multiracial family, and I tell my children that we are part of the larger human family. When we speak of loss of life, I don't restrict the value of human life to that of my own country, because this larger human family is important to me, to my children, and to the cultures from which they come.

I want to talk to you about it because I think there are people who have not been represented here — the people of the Darfur region. I came here to bring them into the discussion and since 2004, when I was first in Darfur, I have worn this necklace around my neck. It was given to me by a woman named Halima. She was wearing it when her village was attacked and when her baby son was torn from her arms and murdered. Three of her five children were similarly killed on that day, and her husband, too. But Halima survived, and she gave me this talisman for my protection. I could offer her no protection, and Halima clasped my two hands and asked me to tell people what is happening in Darfur: "Tell them we will all be slaughtered, tell them we need help."

Since that moment, I have conducted my life with Halima and the courageous people in Darfur who are facing terrible atrocities as we speak. And it isn't only Darfur. Now we're looking at Congo and other places, and I do think being a human being involves being responsible. I tell my children, with knowledge comes responsibility. But for the most part our world leaders don't reflect that principle at all, and I'm not sure that that was reflected fully on this stage by everyone. I do feel if we know that horrific things are happening, that we must then do our utmost, and nothing less than that, to address them with whatever means are available. And I leave it to you, because I do think this is a defining moment. Who are we?

Elie Wiesel wrote: "What astonished us after the torment, after the tempest, was not that so many killers killed so many victims, but that so few cared about us at all." We have to decide whether we are among the few or among the many.

RICK HILLIER: My remarks will be brief. You know, it is soldiers who guarantee democracy, not politicians. It is soldiers who guarantee freedom of speech, not reporters. It is the flag-draped coffin of the soldier that we'll see if we don't get those interventions right. I agree with interventions, if you can guarantee that you have a strategy in place with which you are going to achieve an effect that will last beyond the duration of a six- month tour or a twelve-month rotation. Without a strategy your actions are incoherent and short-term.

Actions and strategies are also susceptible to being hijacked by everyone who comes into that theatre, and by everyone with an opinion — nothing was more frightening to me as commander than the seventy-two-hour visitor who arrived on the ground, instantly assessed everything that they saw, and pierced through the complexities of the situation with a simple solution which was invariably wrong. Institutions like the UN are not capable of giving us the direction, the support, the synergy, the coherence in the international community. I think we've shown that here during this debate.

We do not have the right capacities and capabilities, we don't have government in a box, we don't have developmental organizations that can work to improve a region and help its people. I'm not talking about one or two individuals, I'm not talking about drive-by Ph.D. students. I'm talking about a deployable capability, not somebody who can work only out of the loan hospital or loan school, valuable as that might be.

We do not have the robustness of will in our society to support a long-term mission. I know that as Chief of Defence I always felt that before our first soldier stepped foot on that hostile foreign soil, Canadians had better be stepping with them. We do not have the capacities or the capabilities to develop the expertise in the short term. Yes, we can do it in the long term, but there all kinds of things which unfortunately do occur and for which we are ill-prepared. I give you the example of trying to remove toy guns from the streets of Kabul. Children were using guns to point at our soldiers and we had some dangerous incidents. The soldiers were concerned about this, so we offered prizes for kids to turn in toy guns. In Afghanistan a toy gun is one that is not working; they look very real, and we quickly realized that we were collecting more toy guns than existed in Afghanistan. In fact, guns were being brought in from Pakistan and turned in to the staff troops in Afghanistan.

We don't always understand all of those things that need to be in place before an operation. You simply don't build a team on the run if you're going to be successful. The NATO response has almost always been a complete failure at getting countries to ante up the necessary forces. And without that kind of support, we do not have the moral right to ask our young men and women to go somewhere and do something for which they might pay with their lives, and at the same time not have the effect of saving lives on the other end.

GARETH EVANS: President George W. Bush once famously said to Senator Joe Biden that he didn't do nuance. I think both John Bolton and Rick Hillier have shown tonight that they'd rather learn something from the master in that respect. I think it is a pity that we spent so much of this debate talking past each other about absolutes and about alternatives which are not the real alternatives we face in a world where mass atrocity crimes are an all-too-present reality, and for which we have to struggle to find collective solutions.

When we talk about ending man-made humanitarian crises we're not talking about conflicts generally, we're not talking about human rights violations generally. We're talking about quite a small subset of really tough, really ugly cases where governments — either because of their unwillingness or their incapacity — are allowing or are themselves perpetrating terrible crimes.

We, the international community, have to think about what our responses to those situations are going to be, and in that respect all the options have to be on the table. Diplomatic persuasion, the use of economic sanctions and incentives, the use of legal instruments, and, yes — ultimately, of course, we have to keep open the option of military force.

But let's be nuanced in our understanding of this issue.

Military force is only one option, and really the most extreme measure of addressing humanitarian crises, and it is something we should only agree to because of the stakes that are involved — not the least of which is the blood of our own kids. We have to be very cautious about ever embarking on military missions, but that shouldn't stop us from doing other things that don't involve that kind of traumatic choice.

This involves an exercise of collective will to put in place the preventative strategies, to put in place the reactive strategies, to put in place the helicopters that are needed in Darfur. These things do make a difference. In the end, it's about more than national interest, though of course national interest matters, and we've tried to explain on our side how national interest factors in.

But it can't just be a debate about that. It has to be, as Mia has said so well, about our common humanity, and about our obligation simply as human beings not to stand by and watch our fellow human beings suffer unutterable, unbearable horrors. That is our obligation as international citizens. That is why we have to do everything within our capacity to get these situations right, to prevent them, and to react to them when they occur. That's why it's so important for countries like Canada to maintain the finest traditions of peacekeeping that have made Canada such stars in the international community.

SUMMARY: Bolton and Hillier must have been convincing, as the pre-debate vote was 77 percent in favour of the resolution, 23 percent against with the post-debate vote shifting to 68 percent in favour and 32 percent against.

FOREIGN AID

Be it resolved foreign aid does
more harm than good.

Pro: Dambisa Moyo and Hernando de Soto
Con: Paul Collier and Stephen Lewis

June 1, 2009

FOREIGN AID

INTRODUCTION: The June 2009 Munk Debate asked whether, in trying to do good, well-intentioned people in the developed world are actually making matters worse for people who live in developing economies. The debate resolution was as follows: Be it resolved foreign aid does more harm than good. The panel of experts assembled included the Zambian author of the controversial book *Dead Aid*, Dambisa Moyo; Peruvian economist, author, and President of the Institute for Liberty and Democracy [ILD], Hernando de Soto; Canadian politician, activist, and co-founder of AIDS-Free World, Stephen Lewis; and British author and Professor of Economics at Oxford University, Paul Collier.

Moyo and de Soto argued the pro side while Collier and Lewis took on the con arguments. Both Moyo and de Soto wasted no time in pointing out that the two anti-aid debaters were from the developing world, whereas those convinced the trodden path — which has obviously not worked on all fronts — was the one to continue along were from the West. De Soto focused on the importance of property rights in helping individuals — and nations — gain financial ground and stability. Moyo said that treating Africans and others in developing countries like children was what kept them living in poverty in the first place and only served to perpetuate an already vicious cycle.

Much of the evening's debate pivoted around the arguments in Moyo's book — released just before the event and the subject of many headlines and editorials. And while everyone agreed that the risk of aid money being stolen by dictators and rogue leaders or otherwise going astray was always present, Lewis and Collier felt that eradicating malaria, AIDS, and other diseases was too great a necessity to ignore and that therefore aid had to continue, regardless of potential corruption. De Soto stressed that all four of the debaters believed in helping the developing world, but that it was a question of doing so effectively. He also reminded the audience that immediate aid in a crisis (such as an earthquake or tsunami) was a very different thing from continually flooding money into various global hot spots.

RUDYARD GRIFFITHS: I'm going to ask Stephen Lewis to begin.

STEPHEN LEWIS: Thank you, Rudyard, and fellow colleagues on this debating panel. This morning, Dambisa Moyo and I did a dry run for this debate on *The Current*, on CBC Radio. It was pointed in places, but effortlessly congenial. The simple truth is that Dambisa Moyo has written a book called *Dead Aid* that frames this debate. The book raises a number of interesting issues. I disagree with much of it. I find many of the statistics suspect and at times misleading. But I have none of the jugular instincts that some of her more frenzied detractors have displayed.

Aid to Africa has been wantonly abused over the decades. It has sustained countless despots of the most hideous variety. It has been an engine for corruption, although no more an engine than private capital. It has also been used by international financial institutions — under the guise of structural adjustment programs — to do great damage to Africa's social sectors. But there's an important distinction to be made. All of this says nothing about the intrinsic nature of aid itself. It says everything about donor governments, multinational corporations, and the World Bank and the International Monetary Fund [IMF], who were perfectly content to use aid in the most manipulative and destructive ways imaginable. It takes two to orchestrate dictators, corruption, and Reaganomics. In those particulars, there is some agreement.

What Dambisa Moyo's book fails to acknowledge, I say respectfully, is the huge impact aid has had on the humanitarian imperative. Millions of people living with HIV/AIDS wouldn't be alive today without aid money for antiretroviral drugs; millions of children have been immunized against fatal diseases; over 30 million additional African children are in schools since the year 2000; there has been a modest reduction in extreme poverty, from 58 percent to 51 percent, between 1999 and 2007; 12 million orphans have been given food; and malaria death rates have been cut in half in countries like Rwanda and Ethiopia over the course of two years because of insecticide-treated bed nets. I could go on ad infinitum. These are examples of aid, aid that gets to the grassroots, aid that transforms open communities. It is no small matter, it is no Band-Aid. And, of course, aid does much more.

Dambisa Moyo makes the point that Botswana is the best example of an African government that is democratic in character. The Botswanan government uses a modern approach that is a mix of investment and free markets to build a strong economy. But what she doesn't mention is that Botswana has diamonds. And what is also not said is that, a few years ago, Botswana had the highest prevalence rate of HIV/AIDS in the world — almost 40 percent of the population between the ages of 15 and 49 are infected. The former President of Botswana, Festus Gontebanye Mogae, actually used the word "extinction" when talking about the future of Botswana. What saved Botswana? Aid. What made it possible for Botswana to transition to a vibrant mixed economy? Aid. In the last decade, aid to Africa and elsewhere has become much more focused, monitored, and intelligently applied.

Oddly enough, Dambisa Moyo's book feels curiously out of date. She remains unhappy and unrepentantly suspicious of aid playing any useful role, urgently looking forward to the day when it is removed from the agenda. So her book contains a number of alternative prescriptions that we'll discuss during this debate. Dambisa Moyo suggests that African governments should raise money by issuing bonds on the capital market. I ask: What markets? A year ago, perhaps this would have been a good prescription. Now, hardly a chance. Capitalism has proved itself a touch quixotic — not to say mean, brutish, and ugly. Dambisa Moyo suggests Africa secure foreign direct investment [FDI]. But it's not available. Try as Africa might, secure foreign direct investment has never been available. Africa's share of world FDI is now one percent. And it is not for lack of trying. The countries are too small, the regional groupings ineffectual, the sense of risk overwhelming.

Dambisa Moyo says trade is the answer. Who can disagree? But the current trade negotiation round of the World Trade Organization [WTO] — the Doha Development Agenda [DDA] — is in collapse, and there is not the slightest sign that the United States or Europe is prepared to relinquish agricultural subsidies in order to give African agriculture a chance to export. These are grand designs, but they don't work in practice. I'm a socialist. I'm an expert in grand designs that don't work in practice. Dambisa Moyo believes that China is Africa's salvation. I don't share the same enthusiasm for China as Africa's new neo-colonial master. To do Dambisa Moyo justice, there are more options, ranging from microcredit, to remittances, to savings. But I have to say that, given the state of the world's economy, we're going to need aid for a very long time. The effort should be to make aid more effective, not to expunge it from the balance sheet.

I share the same sense of anxiety, frustration, and rage about the future of Africa, and I'm especially concerned about the future of the next generation of whom Dambisa Moyo speaks. I worry greatly about the quality of political leadership in Africa. I worry even more about the world losing interest in Africa, and I don't think that celebrities are the answer. Believe it or not, I have been going back and forth from the African continent for close to fifty years, and I have nothing but admiration for the intelligence, sophistication, and resilience of the grassroots, especially among the women of Africa. There has to be a way of getting aid into the hands of the grassroots and into the hands of civil society. We have to concentrate on opening doors to other economic designs and transforming the continent. That's where aid continues to do far more good than harm.

RUDYARD GRIFFITHS: Thank you, Stephen. Hernando, please begin with your opening statement.

HERNANDO DE SOTO: Who can disagree with Stephen Lewis? We all believe in aid. It's even a religious precept. It's in the Koran and it's in the Bible. What we are really talking about is whether aid, as it is structured today, causes more harm than it does good. Obviously, it does good. We heard a case for it. But what is the objective of aid?

The objective of aid is essentially to act as a seed, a first seed, a stimulus to begin development so that the Third World can operate like the First World. How does that work? Well, it's about capital. You need capital, obviously. There's nothing in this city [Toronto] that indicates that you don't need capital. You need credit and capital. At the same time, you need a government that ensures that things don't get guided one way or tied up in monopolies. There are three problems that exist in regard to these matters:

first of all, how do you raise capital if you are a developing country? Second, how do you help your poor? Is the sub-prime market a solution? And third, how do you untie aid and how do you get rid of monopolies? Let's begin with the first problem, capital.

How do you raise capital? Take, for example, a Canadian company or a U.S. company. Imagine you are running a U.S. company and you find petroleum in Peru. You get a concession. You ask the government to give you a property right on the land. You get your property right, but you don't trust the Peruvian government, so you have to appeal to your own government — and that's where it begins, because the property right is government-supported — to sign a bilateral investment treaty between the United States and Peru, where the rules of the game are set. In that bilateral investment treaty, you bind the developing country to the facts, aid, and property rights involved. Labour and legislation can no longer change the basis of that treaty. You then present this to an overseas private investment corporation and you tell them to confirm the property right and let the investment corporation know that the U.S. government is behind your company if the Peruvians do something questionable. Then you go to the Multilateral Investment Guarantee Agency [MIGA] for a guarantee and put Peru on notice that they have to honour their agreements. Then, with that property right, which you couldn't have acquired in Canada or the United States, basic taxes and labour are tied up, and there are no exceptions under any circumstances; you go to the capital markets and say, "Have I got a title for you." And that's where the money comes from.

There is no such thing as money or capital without a property right. Money is received when something is given in exchange, such as a guarantee. Then, the company starts operating in Peru, with the backing of the United States or a European country. And at that time, out comes the second head of Janus — in Roman mythology, he is the god with two heads. The second head of Janus is no longer the export credit guarantee department and no longer the diplomats, it is the aid system of the United States or of Western Europe which then says, "We're also giving money, by the way, to a lot of people who have indigenous rights. What are you doing here sitting on indigenous people's space?" Then all of a sudden developing countries see two heads. And that second head says, "These are indigenous people. They have the right to roam. You're trespassing." And all of a sudden in countries like Peru, all hell breaks loose. And all hell breaks loose because both sides are being supported.

Now, why doesn't this happen in the U.S. or in Europe? Because the left and the right form one government, and as a result the government is actually able to work things out. Here's where it gets confusing. At home, in Western capitalist countries, you give Treasury positions to politicians on the right and you give aid and ambassadorship positions to politicians on the left. In the U.S. you have Timothy Geithner as the current U.S. Secretary of the Treasury, and you've got Dr. Susan Rice as U.S. Ambassador to the United Nations. You've got Christine Lagarde as the current Minister of Economic Affairs, Industry and Employment of France, and you've got Bernard Kouchner as the current French Minister of Foreign and European Affairs.

Now, this is all great, because the U.S. and European countries have got their act together. But what happens to other nations? This produces what Marx referred to as a social contradiction. And therefore people in the U.S. and European countries are very happy. They have the investments. But poor people are working against the property system, which creates a left versus right discourse, one which is applicable to developed countries, not to developing countries. Just like there are Hutus and Tutsis warring in Somalia, in developed countries the aid system pits left and right against each other. Sub-prime is the same thing. We're all aware of the recession, I don't have to tell you about it. The only thing that's interesting about sub-prime is that while developed countries have given something in the order of about 300 billion dollars to developing countries, as was pointed out by Stephen, developing countries have given developed countries 2 trillion dollars, because our money went to the United States, and to Europe. That's what basically financed the sub-prime. Why did it go there? Developing countries have a higher return on capital and higher interest rates. Our money went to developed countries because you've got property rights. It is much easier to arrange financing in the United States or in the Western world because you've got something to hold on to. In other words, property rights.

The question then becomes, why don't developing countries have property rights? It is due to a world system or bias that is against indigenous people having property rights. Why? Because Canada, the U.S., and Europe feel guilty about their colonial past, and therefore you aren't willing to do for developing countries what you do for your own citizens.

And last but not least, let me finish with a few words about the matter of tied and untied aid. Canadians are a generous people dedicated to helping developing countries, for which we are very grateful. But you haven't seen what you've done. Aid is untied, for example, through your Canadian International Development Agency [CIDA]. But on the other hand, you've got export credit programs that tie that aid to specific regulations. You may support grants for a hydroelectric plant, but you require that we source materials and professional expertise from you. In one case, we receive a small amount of aid that is untied, and in another case we receive a large amount of foreign aid that restricts us to get the best prices possible. That's a contradiction.

RUDYARD GRIFFITHS: A great start to the debate. Paul, you're next.

PAUL COLLIER: I wrote *The Bottom Billion* because the term "bottom billion" was meant to describe sixty low-income countries that have missed out on global prosperity. They have stagnated while other countries prospered, and as a result they've diverged. They've diverged for forty years, and it is a vital matter both for the people living in these societies and for the rest of mankind that instead of diverging they start to catch up. That is the challenge. However it's done, it seems to me fundamental that the bottom billion converge with the rest of mankind. If the next forty years are like the last forty years, we're heading for tragedy.

So what can we in the rich world do? I think there are four policy areas that are important in achieving convergence.

One is security, which we are actually doing, for example, in Afghanistan. Two is trade policy, which Dambisa emphasizes. Three is governance, and the fourth is aid. Aid is part of that spectrum of effective policies. Why aid? Because the fundamental reality of the bottom billion is that these countries are desperately short of capital. That is their defining feature. It's not their only feature, but it's their defining feature. They've got to accumulate capital, and if they have to do that from internal resources only they'll have to cut consumption deeply, and they're already living at the margin of subsistence. So they need international capital, not just aid but public and private capital. Potentially, they're complements. Public capital provides things like the roads and private capital pays for things like trucks.

Now, in Africa, to date, there has been a lot of criticism of public capital. But the reality is that private international capital has also failed. Let's take a couple of examples. The stellar example of private lending to African governments is Nigeria. In the late 1970s and early 1980s, Nigeria was able to borrow quite heavily on international capital markets. International banks provided money, and they didn't care to ask who was borrowing it or how it was going to be used. The money went down the drain. It left Nigeria with a load of international private indebtedness. The big example of foreign direct investment to Africa over the last decade has been to Angola. Is the government of Angola aligned with its citizens? No, it is not. In fact, even in the boom years, the last crazy five years when private capital would go almost anywhere, it went almost anywhere except to the bottom billion. They were just starting at the margins when the whole thing collapsed. Looking forward, don't hold your breath.

So, why did private capital fail to develop Africa? Was it the fault of aid? Of course not. Aid is not that important. Aid is one of the range of policies. It's a marginal benefit. But the idea that it was responsible for the failure of private capital is untenable. There were much deeper problems. For example, there was the resource curse across much of Africa. There was the political paradox that the societies were too large to be a nation — because the politicians hadn't forged a sense of identity — and yet were too small to be viable states. They couldn't reap the benefits inherent in public capital, in public goods. And often opportunities were quite limited. Some of the countries were landlocked. Once China got into global industrial markets it was very hard to compete against China.

I also wrote *The Bottom Billion* to try and create a centre ground between what I regard as theatrically polarized opposing positions. Without a centre ground we cannot get intelligent public policies. Aid can't fix all these problems. The core struggles are internal. In all these societies there are brave people struggling for change. But we can make aid more effective than it has been. Until the fall of the Soviet Union, aid was given for completely non-developmental reasons or agendas. So we've been through a sixteen-year learning process. And over that time there have been some big mistakes. But they are mistakes that can be rectified. We can condition aid not on the policies that governments adopt — we shouldn't tell governments which policies to adopt — but on the governance of those governments. That is, we should be conditioning aid to require governments to be accountable to their own citizens.

And finally, we can use aid much more strategically, linked up with those other policies — security, trade, and governance policies. Let me close with a Canadian example. It concerns Canada's second biggest aid recipient, which is Haiti. Haiti is the classic country in the bottom billion. And the difficult thing in Haiti, which is the provision of security, has been provided by Brazilians, not Canadians. Brazil has 12,000 peacekeeping troops there. The next difficult thing is trade. The U.S. has taken care of that by creating a special trade deal; they have privileged market access to Haiti. And now what's needed is for aid to be targeted on providing the infrastructure that would enable Haiti to benefit from those opportunities. The ball is in Canada's court. That's an example of aid which could be harnessed to generate the jobs that Haiti so badly needs. If that happens, then, finally, the private investors would come in. Private capital can be the solution, but it is going to be built on public capital.

RUDYARD GRIFFITHS: And now Dambisa will give our final opening statement.

DAMBISA MOYO: Thank you very much. I'd like to, first of all, say thank you to the Munk organizers for allowing me, as an African, to say a few words about the state of my continent, even though I'm not a celebrity. I want to begin by saying, ladies and gentlemen, that we are all on the same side. And what do I mean by that?

There are three fundamental points that we all agree on.

First of all, we all agree that Africa cannot rely on aid forever. We can sit here and quibble about whether it will be another five years or ten years or one hundred years, but I think we fundamentally agree that Africa cannot rely on aid forever. Aid is not the optimum solution. The second thing we agree on is, African governments must lead the charge to increasing growth and reducing poverty on the continent. It is not the responsibility of Westerners. It is not the responsibility of celebrities. Yes, we do need the international community to be front and centre alongside African governments, but, ultimately, the responsibility of leading the charge for Africa's future is the responsibility of African governments. The third thing that I believe that we agree on is that aid has and continues to contribute to the dysfunctionality of African states. The point that Stephen mentioned earlier about corruption is not a figment of my imagination, nor is it something of the past.

Just a couple of months ago, the president of Malawi was indicted for stealing aid money. As I speak, the former president of my country, Zambia, is embroiled in a corruption scandal. Aid is contributing to the corruption, and even in the best case scenario it is allowing African governments to abdicate their responsibilities to provide public goods. Governments around the world, like the Canadian government, the American government, the British government, and others are charged and elected to provide public goods. In Africa, however, public goods such as education, health care, infrastructure, and yes, even security, are provided by donors. That is completely unacceptable.

I will point to a comment by a friend of mine from Africa

who said, "Why do we even bother going to stand in the hot sun to vote for these leaders? We should actually be voting for either the Canadian International Development Agency [CIDA] or the United States Agency for International Development [USAID] because ultimately they are the ones who are providing us with the public goods."

I want to remind everyone of the origins of aid. If you go back to the 1960s, you will know that there was a very simple economic law that savings would lead to investment, which in turn would lead to growth. In the absence of savings, poor countries could rely on foreign aid. And remember, if we talk about the 1950s and 1960s, there were newly-founded countries coming out of the colonial period, and there were not a lot of savings in these economies. So the idea was actually a laudable one, after the success of the Marshall Plan. I'll come to the Marshall Plan later. The simple idea was that aid would replace savings, and aid would therefore drive investment and ultimately lead to growth and reduce poverty. The question then becomes, have we seen an increase in growth over the past sixty years — during which over one trillion dollars of aid money has gone from the Western world towards Africa? The answer is no. Have we seen a decline in poverty? The answer is no. Paul Collier himself has talked about the African continent shearing off from the rest of the world. On those two metrics alone, the aid model has failed. How did this happen? Let me count the ways. I actually had a top ten list of reasons why aid doesn't work, but I'm only going to go through a handful of them.

First, aid fuels corruption, which is obvious. And, by the way, these are not my words, this is the conclusion of the

World Bank, the International Monetary Fund, and from numerous academic studies about how and what aid does in poor and developing countries. Second, aid encourages inflation. Third, it leaves African countries and other developing countries with significant debt burdens that they cannot repay. Another ill effect is that it kills off the export sector. Fifth, it induces social unrest, because remember, the aid money is pooling at the top to governments. Sixth, aid kills entrepreneurship, and ultimately it disenfranchises African citizens. Our governments spend their time courting and catering to donors. They do not care about what their citizens have to say. In other words, it's the reverse Boston Tea Party. No representation without taxation.

Governments in developed countries respond to their people and provide public goods simply because they have to rely on the tax base provided by voters. Proponents of aid will argue that there are 2 million Africans on HIV/AIDS drugs and 34 million Africans are going to school. And that's all well and good. I myself sit on charity boards that look specifically at HIV drugs and at providing education. But they neglect three fundamental questions.

First of all, what is going to happen in ten to twenty years when these aid programs are no longer financed? The fact that the United States is facing a 10 percent unemployment rate and has other pressing concerns, and Germany's economy is contracting by up to 6 percent, leads Africans to wonder what is going to happen when these countries are no longer able to finance aid programs. But that is a minor problem.

The second question is: What are African governments

doing with the money that they have? We have just come out of one of the most amazing bull runs in commodity prices. Does anybody care to ask what has happened to that money? No, instead they say, let's just give them more aid. And finally, what exactly is the plan for African governments to deliver on their provision of public goods? Again, nobody wants to know that. The good news is that we actually know what delivers growth and what reduces poverty.

In our lifetime, China has moved 300 million people out of poverty. Did they do this with aid? No, they did it with trade. They did it with foreign direct investments. They relied on the capital markets. By the way, I should mention that a Chinese diplomat said to me, two months ago, "Dambisa, anybody who tells you that the capital markets are closed and that African governments shouldn't bother is ludicrous. And it's usually a Westerner who tells you. If you want to raise capital, come to China, or to the Middle East, we have the money."

We in Africa are looking to create jobs. Enough with the handouts. We are trying to be equal partners on the global stage. We do not want sympathy or pity. We want opportunities. And the only way we are going to succeed is if Westerners stop feeling sorry for Africans and start treating us as equals and adults and not as children.

I'm going to conclude with a comment that a friend of mine from Nigeria made. He said, "Why have you bothered to write this book? It's a complete waste of time, nobody cares." And he added, "You do know why they give aid, don't you? Ultimately, it's because Africa is to development what Mars is to NASA. We spend billions of dollars every year analyzing, researching, quibbling about data, but ultimately, nobody really believes that we're going to live on Mars and nobody believes that Africa is actually going to develop."

RUDYARD GRIFFITHS: I want to offer the two sides the opportunity to rebut some of the things that they've heard in the opening statements. Let's start with Stephen.

STEPHEN LEWIS: It's hard to disagree with what Dambisa says, in particular. There are several African countries that have moved forward, quite remarkably, in the last ten years, in terms of economic growth and internal democracy and democratic elections, and are looking to overcome the reliance on Western aid. I don't take any exception or difference with that. The problem is the transition. The problem is that at this particular moment in time, the evidence does not yet suggest that the trade rules will change, that the foreign direct investment will be available, or that the bond markets will respond. I point out that Ghana had to withdraw its bond renewal because the markets are not available. This is likely to go on for some time. We're fighting for survival en route. These are not marginal questions. We've got millions of people fighting for survival as they move towards a more mixed economy. None of us would deny the legitimacy of that. We have to continue using aid intelligently and effectively. I don't see any way around that. I guess that's the fundamental concern that I have. The dismissal of aid may consign a lot of people to extraordinary risk, without recognizing that it's a necessary part of a transition to a broader and more mixed economy.

RUDYARD GRIFFITHS: Dambisa, in your book you made a somewhat controversial recommendation to turn the aid tap off, and to do so relatively quickly. How do you respond to Stephen's comment that this is a long transition and it seems you want it done relatively quickly? Isn't there a risk of shock therapy? How do you make that transition?

DAMBISA MOYO: First of all, I have been misquoted. I have never said we should switch off the taps immediately. What I have said is, we should be discussing an exit strategy, and we should be aspiring to a time when African governments can start to be weaned off aid. I think the fundamental problem with the aid system is that it's all couched in negatives. And if you actually listen to what Stephen Lewis has just said, it's littered with negatives. It is the poor Africans with HIV and the poor woman who is getting raped. It's the tragedy. I'm here to tell you that there is good news, and we're trying to focus on that good news to significantly transform our continent. Let me share with you a few things.

First of all, there are now sixteen countries in Africa that have credit ratings. They have credit ratings of B minus and above, which are not bad ratings. It's the same rating as Turkey, for example. I do not believe that many African governments would have chosen to take those ratings if they thought that they were going to be worse off with them. We know that Turkey, like many other single B countries around the world, has come to the capital markets. The question is, why are many African countries not even exploring that as an option? They should be.

Second, over 60 percent of the African population is under

the age of twenty-four. This is a young, vibrant, energetic population that desperately wants to be part of the Twitter and Facebook era. I frequently receive messages from people in Africa who are struggling and using their last dime to send me an email, because they are interested in being part of a global community. But they are constantly getting shut out because we prefer to hear from celebrities. The International Monetary Fund is forecasting that Africa is going to grow by 3 percent this year. The sub-Saharan African growth rate is at 3 percent. At a time when, as I said earlier, Germany is talking about contracting by 6 percent, we're seeing 10 percent unemployment perhaps in the U.S. and we are seeing global growth perhaps at 0.5 percent. So it's not such a bad story.

Some people might not even know that there are over fifteen stock markets in Africa right now. Over 85 percent of the stocks that trade on African stock markets are non-commodities. So the notion that Africa is one big commodity play, I think, is again misleading. There are telecommunications stocks, consumer goods stocks, and real estate stocks. The story is there. It is just about changing our mindset. We need to encourage people to speak in positive terms about the continent. Otherwise, how do we expect us to raise young people on a continent when they're constantly being told that they can't do it, they're too poor and they need aid?

RUDYARD GRIFFITHS: Hernando, I'd like you to focus on a single proposition or idea that Stephen or Paul has put forward that you take exception to, and explain to us why.

HERNANDO DE SOTO: To start off with, Paul speaks as if capital were money. There are about 13 trillion dollars' worth of currencies in the world if you add up all the dollars, Swiss francs, euros, etc. Where do credit and capital come from? They are in the form of a lot of paper that has equity — equity, bonds, derivatives, financial instruments. It isn't currency and it isn't money. It is paper that, as you have learned through the recession, is backed by assets. What does backed by assets mean? It means that what really supports paper currency are the underlying assets: it is homes, land, airplanes. It is all recorded, it's all registered.

But in developing countries such as mine or Dambisa's, the assets aren't titled. They are not on paper and they cannot be converted into capital. So it isn't that developing countries don't have capital. They have capital, but it is dead because it isn't — for lack of a better word — paperized. Having said that, you don't have to travel to Zambia or Peru to know what I'm talking about.

But if you want an example close to home, go and visit Indian reservations in Canada. You have got people there who have assets, but they are dead assets that can't be used as collateral. This goes back to the *Indian Act* over 140 years ago. Now you support your Native peoples through aid programs — for whatever guilt reasons. But the effect is to make their assets totally useless by denying your Native peoples of property rights. First they were deprived of property rights, and then they were deprived of their sovereignty. And when sovereignty goes, so does the pride of a people. Sovereignty is the real issue in the Palestinian-Israeli conflict. The solution there is to settle the border dispute. You say once and for all, this is Watusi territory, this is Aztec territory, this is Blackfoot territory. When you restrict sovereignty, people don't like it. And assimilation isn't always the solution, either. You've tried that in Canada. They should have been given property, so that inside their sovereignty they can convert assets into capital.

I appreciate aid enormously. But what I'm also trying to tell you is that aid doesn't give priority to creating property conditions in countries like mine. Instead of encouraging programs that support property rights, we throw money at maintaining tribes and clans. And in the process you end up creating special interest groups that resist any real chance.

I'm not against aid per se. But you in the West created wealth through a comprehensive system of property rights. All we want is the chance to create the same system: a system where we can produce wealth by "pauperizing" our assets.

RUDYARD GRIFFITHS: Let me turn to you, Paul. Are property rights the panacea?

PAUL COLLIER: First of all, let me agree with Dambisa that Africa is a region of economic opportunity for private investment. Recently, I've tried to triangulate three different data sources on rates of return on investment around the world, return on equity, and return on American foreign direct investment abroad. I've also examined the results from surveys of 18,000 manufacturing firms around the world. All three of them show, along with the data, that Africa has the highest return on private capital of anywhere in the world. So there is opportunity in Africa. But now let's juxtapose that with the high rates of return that have been sitting there for the past five years, through the greatest credit bonanza the earth has seen. The credit didn't flow. Now, maybe it is a problem of property rights. But it's actually a bit deeper than that, because property rights will only function as collateral internationally if there are supporting institutions.

I remember talking with someone at a bank in Uganda who said, "Oh, we finally managed to get foreclosure on a piece of land." This person was initially very pleased that the judge for the first time had ordered this asset because of the default. And then they discovered that what we thought was the land on which a factory was built was actually the swamp next to the factory, and that's why they were able to get the claim ordered. The problem is that these institutional difficulties are slow to fix. There aren't quick fixes for them. We've been in this situation before during the 1990s, when the World Bank took the view that they didn't need to finance infrastructure, and then the World Bank disastrously shifted from financing infrastructure to financing a social agenda.

HERNANDO DE SOTO: But sometimes there are quick fixes, Paul. How did Japan, a feudal country in 1945, become one of the most developed countries in the world ? First, it happened because Japan revamped its feudal institutions by protecting property rights, thereby becoming one of the most powerful countries in the world. Second, how do you explain the development in China? Even though China is still run by the Communist Party, it has adopted capitalist principles and protected property rights. That's why they are able to attract vast amounts of private capital and investment from around the world.

PAUL COLLIER: I seem to remember that during the late 1940s there were quite a lot of American troops in Japan.

HERNANDO DE SOTO: Well, how about China, Paul?

PAUL COLLIER: Let me finish my story on the World Bank during the 1990s. The former President of the World Bank, James Wolfensohn, a member of the banking community, believed that infrastructure in Africa was going to be financed by the private banking sector. He believed that there wasn't any role for the World Bank, so the bank closed its lending on infrastructure. And what did Africa get? Did it get a lot of banks coming in and financing infrastructure? No. Eventually China stepped in. But China is a two-edged sword in this context. The Chinese deals are for infrastructure in return for the rights to plunder — and sometimes that's okay and sometimes it isn't. But it is not an example of the replication of the Western banking model. The institutional base to provide big private capital doesn't exist.

HERNANDO DE SOTO: Every country is a special case. There were American troops in Japan, but that is absolutely irrelevant. There are troops in Afghanistan and nothing has happened. There are U.S. troops in Iraq, and nothing has happened. The reason Japan developed is because, in addition to troops, there was a plan. And what I am saying is that one of the things I get from reading about all of the aid programs is that these programs focus on charity and handouts, not real economic development.

PAUL COLLIER: There I agree.

STEPHEN LEWIS: How can you agree? Agreement is betrayal. I am not prepared to sacrifice the African continent for a free market, neo-liberal ideology, which in large measure has not been tested, is unwarranted, and probably won't work. And the truth of the matter is that Africa has not been able to produce the foreign direct investment which many people — surprisingly enough, myself included — have tried desperately over the years to get from the multilateral and multinational world. Trade is closed to Africa. The world is doing everything it can to shut Africa down. If I may make the point, China's oil involvement in Sudan is what sustains the genocide in Darfur. Involvement with China is definitely a pact with the devil. Dambisa has said, "I want to have food on the table for a rural woman." She doesn't want to wait forever, and she can't embrace human rights in the process. And I understand that. It is a powerful, visceral feeling. But the truth of the matter is that with China you never know where you stand, and the abrogation of human rights is so fundamental and so extensive that it may compromise entire nation-states down the road.

All we're saying about aid is that it can help you with infrastructure and agriculture. Aid can put girls into secondary school and then into universities, so that they can then do the work that Dambisa wants countries to do. And I do not consider it negative to say that people are fighting for survival. It is an objective truth, and it seems to me that it is legitimate in concert and in partnership with Africa to assist that survival through the aid process. It is not about being neo-colonial in the process. It is simply about being decent human beings who respond to a dilemma or a predicament in another part of the world, recognizing that in the course of time — and let it be sooner rather than later — those countries have to take over matters that concern them without interference from abroad.

DAMBISA MOYO: Sixty years and one trillion dollars. Aid has not delivered. You do not live on aid in Canada. You are pushing a strategy that has no evidence of working anywhere on earth. There isn't a single country that has meaningfully reduced poverty and achieved long-term economic growth by relying on aid to the extent that African governments rely on aid. And when aid has worked — the Marshall Plan, for example — the interventions have been short, sharp, and finite. Not the open-ended commitments that you are supporting here. With respect to political institutions, democracy, governance, and all of those lovely buzzwords that we like to throw around, the fact of the matter is that we will never get them in Africa until there is a middle class on the ground that can hold governments accountable. It is not good enough to try to shoehorn these types of institutions into a continent where ultimately the governments are not incentivized to cater to their domestic populations.

Let me give you an example: one of the aid darlings, Ethiopia. Everyone wants to give money to Ethiopia. This is the second largest population in sub-Saharan Africa, a country of 100 million people. Ethiopia has a 2 percent mobile phone penetration rate, and there's no reason why you should know the significance of this statistic, but let me give you some colour. In Africa today, the mobile phone penetration rate across the continent is about 30 percent. There are at least thirty countries on earth today where mobile phone penetration rates are more than 100 percent. In other words, there are countries where people have more than one mobile phone. If you go to places like Europe, it is very common. Now, we know how mobile phones can help Africans. For example, in Ghana it is a tool people can use to increase their income. Somebody can use their mobile phone to text into town A and find out how much a cow is worth — say, twenty dollars — and then text to town B and to find out how much a cow is — say, forty dollars. So they would then know to take their cow to town B. Mobile phones are also useful in Kenya, where people are using their phones to get information about when the doctor is coming to their village. However, representatives from Ethiopia, an aid darling, skulk around at the G20 meetings looking for additional aid money. Ethiopia has deliberately chosen not to open its market.

Let me just say this with respect to the question of foreign direct investment. There hasn't been more foreign direct investment in Africa because doing business across Africa is a nightmare. African governments, by and large, are not incentivized to create the environments that support private investment. In some countries, it takes up to two years to get a business licence. I travelled to Rwanda, Kenya, and

Tanzania, three countries that are close to one another. I needed three visas, and I had to change my currency three times. Does this sound like a formula for countries that are interested in encouraging private sector development? No. These countries live and die by donor money. They are not incentivized to do the right thing.

We know what the right thing is. We know what creates jobs. We know that more trade is better than less trade. We know that countries that have relied on foreign direct investment have meaningfully reduced poverty and created growth, and we know that countries that have consistently sat back and relied on aid have underperformed. We know this. Let's not pretend. Let us not make up stories. Let's save the bleeding heart for somebody else. It's time to change.

RUDYARD GRIFFITHS: Hernando, I want you to pick up on something that Stephen Lewis said, because I think it's important. How do the kind of free-wheeling, free market ideas that you've espoused in your writing not represent a doubling down on a capitalist model which has been a little tarnished here in the West in the last eighteen months?

HERNANDO DE SOTO: The first thing is that I do not identify myself as a free-wheeling, neo-liberal. I classify myself as an admirer of socialist form and the free market form of the West. What I'm saying is that these forms are effective in the West. It's not — like this discussion — left or right. There are certain areas that are grey, and Western countries have been able to work things out. Stephen mentioned Darfur. And yes, the West has to help. But how did the situation in Darfur come about? As a matter of fact, since 1991, there have been fifteen African civil wars and insurrections over territory and property rights. The civil war is essentially about tribes fighting over defined pieces of territory.

Western countries emphasize everything except that which makes them great, which is their rule of law. Don't forget how violent your eighteenth and nineteenth centuries were. How did the West overcome it? Is there something about the Anglo-Saxon character that allowed you to get over it? Or is it the fact that after the Gold Rush and after the conquest of the west, a social contract with clear definitions of property was established? And, by the way, that social contract was developed by both the left and the right. I don't want to get dragged into this argument about neo-liberal and other labels. I admire the ability of the West to make both the left and the right function in tandem, which you've been able to do so well inside your countries. And, yet, when you go into other countries, you fight, because it gives you a sense of guilt towards your own indigenous peoples. Because you haven't been able to sort out the conflicts between sovereignty and property. When you do, you'll also be able to sort out Africa. The wars in Africa are about territory.

But there is a problem with the term "property rights." You say "property rights" and everybody thinks, "My God, it's Ronald Reagan!" "Property rights" is simply the structure of law that sets out ownership, so that Africans can live in peace and no longer depend on the West.

RUDYARD GRIFFITHS: Paul, why do you think that the China/India model isn't necessarily open to a lot of African countries?

PAUL COLLIER: China and India share two characteristics which the bottom billion doesn't have. One is that they are both huge, and big societies tend to be better governed. We'd like to think small is cozy, but actually small is personalized power and a lot of corruption. Power has to be institutionalized in India and in China, and that helps. The other thing is that neither China nor India are rich in natural resources, and natural resources tend to produce a lot of bad governance. These are the features that are at the heart of the problem of the bottom billion, rather than aid. And there have been examples of aid cut-offs. Zimbabwe, for example, has not received a lot of aid in the last decade; it's not exactly a model of improved governance.

DAMBISA MOYO: Zimbabwe received 300 million dollars from the U.K. and U.S. governments in 2006. That's 300 million U.S. dollars.

PAUL COLLIER: They have received very little aid in recent years, and similarly Eritrea has tried to cut itself off from aid, but Eritrea is a tragedy of personalized abuse of power. Dambisa started to describe the process of no representation without taxation, but actually the process which forged effective states — which was the process in Europe — was a much more brutal process than just taxation. The process that forged effective states in Europe was military rivalry between political elites in different countries. In order to win the international military struggle, they had to have high taxation to pay for their militaries. And then there was a Darwinian process in which the countries that managed to build the most effective tax system won the international struggle. Europe paid a horrendous price. And we can't possibly wish that process of international struggle on Africa. In other words, we can understand how the West managed to build effective states and Africa hasn't. We have to find a different and better way to effective statehood.

HERNANDO DE SOTO: What about South Korea? What about Hong Kong? What about Switzerland? What about Liechtenstein and Benelux? These countries don't have to be big to be governed effectively. Why define something different when here in Canada you've got something that works? Why not imitate something that works?

PAUL COLLIER: Countries that are small, poor, and resource-rich have really big challenges in producing an effective state. Some are able to do it. Botswana has managed it. To my mind that shows how tremendously good the early leadership of Botswana was. Social science doesn't observe hard and fast laws. It works by tendencies. The tendency is for small, poor, and resource-rich countries to fall into a trap. These countries are in a cul-de-sac. And that's the situation in Africa. It is not due to aid. Aid is a weak instrument that we use to try and get out of that cul-de-sac.

HERNANDO DE SOTO: We are not against humanitarian aid. We are against the negative externalities that some aid brings with it. We have already said that. Who could be against charity? We are against the negative externalities of aid, and we are trying to improve the system. On that we all agree.

RUDYARD GRIFFITHS: Dambisa, you know Paul Collier writes quite eloquently in his book *The Bottom Billion* about some of these large structural factors, including the size of the country, good or poor neighbours, the degree to which natural resources are prevalent or not, and the degree to which they have sea access or not. You offer an interesting rebuttal in your book, *Dead Aid*. Why is it that the structural factors won't necessarily overwhelm the types of reform that you're proposing?

DAMBISA MOYO: I'm not sure which rebuttal you mean. It's such an excellent book that there are certainly many rebuttals. The obvious thing is incentives. The West is a society of incentives. The governments and institutions are incentivized to do the right thing. Individuals in the West are incentivized to do certain things. And to the extent that those things fall out of line from the common good, the legal system steps in to manage your behaviour. In Africa, and certainly in the aid system, there is a situation where the donors are incentivized to give money, even though they are aware that the money is not going to the right places. And African governments are incentivized to take the money because it is easier for them to take the money. Who wants to travel around the world pitching bonds to a thousand pension funds when all international investors do is rip you apart and ask you what your agenda is? Why do that when all you have to do is pick up the phone and call the World Bank for the next cheque?

The question is, how do we get African governments to be incentivized to do the right thing? As I said earlier, African governments have to be on board. They have to get involved. I come from a landlocked country of 10 million people. But in the southern African context we are talking about 200 million people. How do I get my government to be incentivized to be part of the southern African community in a credible and meaningful way that would work to improve the livelihoods of our society? The fact of the matter is, as long as the government has a credible system of aid coming through year in and year out, whether there's a credit crisis or not, African governments are never going to be fully incentivized to do the right thing. With respect to aid, we have tried many different interventions.

In the 1960s, we had aid for infrastructure. In the 1970s, we had aid for poverty and growth. In the 1980s, we had aid structured for adjustment and stabilization programs. In the 1990s, we had aid for democracy and governance. And now, in the 2000s, we have glamour aid, where everyone feels like they can adopt a child and start running around the continent with a new scheme. We are not addressing the fundamental point. We will never address the fundamental point by giving money to anyone for free — without any credible conditions. We will have a situation where we get the institutions and the growth and the reduction of poverty that we're seeking. We know this. We know what China has done. We know what India has done, and Brazil and Russia. Even on the African continent itself, there are countries such as South Africa and Botswana, countries that do not rely on aid to the extent that most African states do. Let's not try and reinvent the wheel. We know what works. Change your attitude with respect to Africa.

I'm not letting you — the donor nations — off the hook. I'm not saying go to your homes and don't do anything with respect to Africa. I'm saying that we know how to intervene. We can provide capital in terms of microfinancing, support entrepreneurship, encourage African governments to open their markets, encourage governements to hold African policy-makers to account, and treat Africans as equals as opposed to children. If we get past that, I'm telling you, my continent will rise and be an equal partner on the global stage.

STEPHEN LEWIS: Let's look at a couple of countries which are important. Look at Botswana. For several years in this century, Botswana was receiving four times more aid per capita than the average across the African continent. Why? Because aid made it possible for Botswana to survive the force of the pandemic, and Botswana was able to develop and move to economic growth. The two worked in tandem. Rwanda, a country of which Dambisa is particularly fond — for good reason, because the President of Rwanda, Paul Kagame, summoned his entire cabinet when her book was launched in Rwanda and they all bought copies. And they gave me some aid money in payment for it. I'm going to avoid the obvious. Paul Kagame has been public in his support for Dambisa's thesis. In fact, he wrote an op–ed in the *Financial*

Times in which he complimented Dambisa on the book. And he wrote that he wanted to reach the day when Rwanda is free of aid — a perfectly legitimate objective. Let me point out that over 50 percent of Rwanda's present budget comes from aid. Is Kagame happy about that? No. Does he want to release himself from it? Yes. Does he recognize that it's not possible to do that in a peremptory and abrupt fashion, that if you're going to build a society with economic and fiscal integrity you have to use aid as the transition point even when you've got a country that is pretty autocratic, which everybody agrees has happened within Rwanda? Yes. And there's no avoiding that.

You can't talk in abstractions about where African states will get the money. Aid is used to move those states to self-reliance, to become strong economic entities, and aid is necessary for the transition. Has aid been misused and abused? Sure. I regret that deeply. Has it been used by corrupt oligarchs? Absolutely. I regret that completely. Is the West bereft? There is Citibank, AIG, a number of others, let alone [Bernie] Madoff, that come to mind. I was in the British parliament when the speaker resigned, and I almost had traumatic apoplexy. I went into total withdrawal because the members of parliament had siphoned off so much public money. It bothers me when Africa is singled out as the culprit of corruption. Alas, corruption is an infection internationally which must be dealt with. You would think that it wouldn't happen in modern nation-states. But it does. And I genuinely believe, Dambisa, we're not so far apart on this. I want to see the economic growth as much as you do, but I don't know how they get there without some transitional income to sustain them. And that's what's missing.

DAMBISA MOYO: So you're right to bring up Rwanda. I really wish that instead of me sitting here, as merely a citizen of a continent of a billion people that nobody seems to really care about, it were a president from Africa sitting here explaining their plan. Rwanda is an interesting case. Actually, over 70 percent of their budget is aid money, and frankly, given what happened and the manner in which the world turned away when they were in the middle of the genocide fifteen years ago, it would suggest to me that they have every reason to guilt trip the whole world. Former U.S. President Bill Clinton still feels bad about that. The Rwandan government could guilt trip us and keep asking for ever more money.

So the question is, what is it that President Kagame sees that puts him at the forefront of the people talking about the ills of aid? I'll share with you what he told me — I'm going to paraphrase his comments about this whole system. His arguments are mainly philosophical, whereas I have approached aid from an economic perspective. But I think it's very important to give you his key point, which is that any country in Africa or around the world that would sit back and rely on aid has not experienced genocide. They have not experienced a situation where the Western world, the donor community, turns around and walks away. And the fact of the matter is that, by voting for the motion that aid is a good thing and aid programs should continue, you're actually asking us as Africans to continue to sit back and rely on your tax money to sustain ourselves. We cannot do that. We will remain vulnerable. We cannot do that, especially when you have your own budgetary pressures in the West. Look at the U.S. borrowing from China. The U.S. doesn't have money either.

STEPHEN LEWIS: I want to make it clear that I chat with Kagame, too. We've had very serious conversations about the genocide in Rwanda, and I understand his reluctance to be reliant on aid in the aftermath. But let me make another analogy. You've got President Ellen Johnson Sirleaf, the first woman elected president in an African nation. She is the President of Liberia and she wrote a stirring op-ed for the *Washington Post*, saying that it would be a terrible mistake to cut back on aid for countries like Liberia when they are attempting to transition into modern nation-states. She is the leader of an African country that is coming out of conflict, and she understands the need for aid. But a lot of countries in Africa are coming out of conflict. And it is terribly important to recognize that they all understand that aid is useful during the transition, just as it was for Botswana, which didn't experience the conflict — just as it is for Ghana, Senegal, Mali, Tanzania, Kenya, Uganda, and Lesotho. All of these countries rely on aid to get them where they want to go. Please don't disparage it as a vehicle of emancipation.

DAMBISA MOYO: So when is the exit? It has been sixty years.

STEPHEN LEWIS: You have to speak to both the right and the left.

RUDYARD GRIFFITHS: We're going to have to move on to a question from the Munk Debates web site. "Are web sites like kiva.org — Kiva is a microfinancing/person-to-person investment site — really the silver bullet? Some argue their benefits are exaggerated and they have their own negative dynamics. Are these concerns substantiated?"

PAUL COLLIER: First of all, there is no silver bullet. As these countries enter middle income, the transformation is going to be a hard struggle. The Kiva web site, yes, of course is a good thing. I think the benefits of microfinance are real, but they are exaggerated. The truth is that these countries will develop predominantly through larger organizations rather than through microfinancing. There's a lot of romance around the micro, both in the rural areas and in the urban areas. In many ways, rural peasants and these sorts of tiny businesses of the informal sector are a consequence of the larger failure to get the formal urban economy growing. That is what happened in East Asia. The urban formal economy took off. To get that takeoff we need platforms of good infrastructure which the private sector is not willing to pay for. So we need public capital to lead that process.

RUDYARD GRIFFITHS: We have another question from the web site for Hernando specifically. "Is the trade-off between free markets and foreign aid really a false choice, a false dichotomy? Can't we have both in equal amounts?"

HERNANDO DE SOTO: Oh, absolutely. And let me tie it in with what I was about to say. I'd like to repeat that I haven't talked about cutting off aid anywhere. What we have said, and I think that's the emphasis of both Dambisa and myself, is that aid has got to have clear objectives.

Let's look at the numbers. The West gives 10 billion dollars in concessional aid a year to developing countries. In terms of overseas development assistance, which comes with many guarantees, it's about 105 billion dollars. If you add the private sector, assisted by export guarantees and others, it is about 472 billion dollars. Now, here is what happens, and this is the kind of thing that I would like people to understand. It is that the market offers the capacity and the possibility of comparing. I admire this; I see it working in Canada, and I see it working in Europe. And although I am so grateful that you have decided to untie your aid, so that you can use Canadian funds to fund projects that happen elsewhere, we are still talking about 10 billion dollars. What interests me is the other 500 billion.

And let me tell you how that's tied up, and it isn't through finance. The way it's tied up is that aside from the people giving charity and doing good and wonderful work all over the world, there are other sectors which are called export credit guarantees. You've got *La compagnie française d'assurance pour le commerce extérieur* [Coface], the [U.K.] Export Credits Guarantee Department [ECGD], and other organizations that give concessional aid to each developing country and fund studies on how a particular country is going to build a hydroelectric plant or their plans for infrastructure or a meat-packing factory, whatever it is. So they have their local company supervising the studies. Of course, what does a Belgian engineer do when he or she draws up the specifications? They get the specifications from Belgians. A French person calls up *ses compagnons*, and the British call up their friends, because that's where they get their information. The engineers write up the specifications and they tender them. Fair and square, according to the World Bank. And overall, the average surcharge is 60 percent. Let me tell you, using figures from the Pakistani National Development Commission, prices for projects coming from Germany could go up 392 percent for using so-called assistance aid, over those in the market. And in the case of Italy, it is 240 percent. In the case of Japan, it would be 123 percent. It isn't that the German government wanted to do this, or that the Japanese government wanted to, it is that the private sector will always seek profit. Countries receiving aid must be allowed to shop for the best prices in an open transparent process. Make aid compete with the private sector. Let's get the price out in the open instead of tying it.

RUDYARD GRIFFITHS: The next question here is from someone writing about Haiti and saying that Haiti is a country in which Canada has invested a lot. It has various national and other connections to Canada. What are the one or two specific policy prescriptions you prescribe for Haiti? Let me start with Dambisa, and then I'll go to Paul.

DAMBISA MOYO: I think Haiti is another example of the failure of an aid system. People want jobs. It's as simple as that. They don't want charity. They don't want handouts or sympathy or guilt or pity or whatever you want to call it. They want jobs. The question then becomes, how do we get a situation where we can create jobs in a place like Haiti? There have been a number of interventions over the years. A lot of them have been aid-based interventions in places like Haiti. Of course, the political system there is unstable, but again I would argue that is essentially an artifact of the aid model. And when we start thinking away from the aid model, the obvious alternative is the free market system, which has, whether we like it or not, delivered wealth. I refer you to U.S. President Barack Obama's inauguration speech. If I may paraphrase, he did say that the free market system is still the best system in creating wealth and creating freedom. So we might all be tempted to throw out the baby with the bathwater, but let us not forget that the free market system has still delivered over the long term. And I would argue that, unfortunately, this is not the system that is applied to places like Haiti. We continue to push aid. It is the easy thing to do. We just send them a little money and keep them out of our hair and, unfortunately, that's part of the problem.

RUDYARD GRIFFITHS: Paul, Haiti is one of the countries that you're advising right now, is that correct?

PAUL COLLIER: Yes. I was in Haiti a few weeks ago. I addressed 250 businessmen and women there. I got a standing ovation and someone said to me, "You realize that 80 percent of the entire private wealth of Haiti is in this room." It is a small economy. But it is a classic case of a country that has not been able to develop its own resources. Haiti needs effective international support across the full range of policies, otherwise it's in a cul-de-sac. Until recently, Haiti hasn't had a full range of intelligent international policies. Haiti has had the politics of gestures rather than effective intervention.

But at last in Haiti, the international community is getting it right. The hardest thing has been the Brazilians going in and securing the peace. They've been there five years, and have made the difference between large-scale violence and order. Without order, you can't do anything. But that's been done. The next thing was to create some economic opportunities. And Dambisa is entirely right. The key thing in Haiti is jobs. Jobs for young people. It has one of the fastest growing populations in the world, and Haitians need jobs. There aren't any. We know how to create jobs in the private sector through areas like manufacturing. But Haiti is not competitive against China. And that's where trade policy comes in. America has given ten years' guaranteed privileged access to its markets for Haitian products. And now with that privilege of access — and Haiti has had it for eighteen months — nothing has happened.

Why has nothing happened? Because the private firms that could have moved in were saying that the infrastructure was terrible. Would the private sector fund the infrastructure? No, the private sector is actually waiting for public sector guarantees to fund the infrastructure. Now, the public sector, which basically means Canada, has a choice as to whether to continue with the old aid agenda, or switch the agenda to financing the infrastructure, which would then unlock private investment. That is the strategic use of aid, and that's Canada's decision now. But if

Canada and the international community give up on Haiti, if the Brazilians go home, if the U.S. says, "Forget it, we are going to give the same trade deal to everyone," Haiti will plunge further into despair. So we have an opportunity, as an effective international community, to make Haiti's future very different from Haiti's past. I hope we take it.

RUDYARD GRIFFITHS: Hernando, I want to hear from you, because I believe that the government of Haiti is looking at what you're doing at your institute. And they're applying some of those ideas to the challenges that they're facing on the ground.

HERNANDO DE SOTO: Absolutely. First of all, Paul, I would request that you thank the Brazilians and the Peruvians, because the other troops in Haiti are Peruvian. Secondly, what I think is important, before getting into economics, is the politics of it. Haiti needs to be able to represent its own people. There is a tendency in the West to be outfoxed by the Third World. If a Third World country elects a parliament or establishes an executive branch or a judiciary, the West sends in Jimmy Carter to say we did it right. It's a lot deeper than that. In the West, parliamentarians respond to specific districts. And they have got to address the questions of a specific constituency. In Haiti, like in all of Latin America, there are no real district elections for politicians. They come from party lists, and what happens therefore is that the parties do not know or respond to the grassroots. They respond to the politicians.

So, I would say a fundamental reform in Haiti would be to

get real democracy. We can't invent it. The West has already invented it. So let's imitate what you've got, which is local representation and decentralization, which is making sure that politicians govern according to feedback, which is where we in the Third World are really going wrong.

Third, I think it is important to understand that Haiti isn't alone. It's one of two countries on an island called Española, where, you may remember, Christopher Columbus landed. And one of the interesting things is that if you look at the border between Haiti and the Dominican Republic, you'll notice that the Dominican Republic is all green. And when you look at the Haitian border, you can see a straight line and it's all brown on the Haitian side. What's the difference? The difference is that President Leonel Fernández and the Dominican government listened to our advice and created property rights. Dominican citizens are actually able to plant seeds, knowing that it is an investment that will pay off, because they own the land. They don't have that in Haiti, so the first thing they need is a system of property rights.

I remember when I first met Jean-Bertrand Aristide, the former President of Haiti, and the current President of the Republic of Haiti, René Garcia Préval. The first thing they said was that, because of their socialist origins, they were going to implement agrarian reform. They had had enough of former President François "Papa Doc" Duvalier, former President Jean-Claude "Baby Doc" Duvalier, and their high-flung friends. They wanted to establish a system of distribution in Haiti. They failed because they didn't know who owned what. How can you distribute and redistribute if there isn't a property records system? There's only one way to do it. Record them. Then you can decide whether someone has too much or too little. First of all, give them property. When you do that, what will actually happen? According to our evaluation, the value of extra-legal assets in Haiti, both in the urban and in the rural sector, is no less at replacement value. If you own that hut, what would it take to rebuild it? We're not even going to put in market value, just replacement value, which is about 15 to 20 billion dollars. What's 15 to 20 billion dollars? It's forty times more than what North Americans have offered Haiti. So it goes by internal reform.

There's nothing wrong with Brazilian troops, there's nothing wrong with Peruvian troops, there's nothing wrong with Canadian aid. Just stop trying to invent the wheel when you've already got the wheel at home and you don't even apply it to your own indigenous people. If you don't want to do that, then don't do that. But please treat us, in the Third World, as white people.

STEPHEN LEWIS: Let me plug Hernando's book *The Mystery of Capital* because at the back of the book there are some absolutely fascinating graphs which measure the worth of properties in various countries, extrapolated to total worth, showing that this property transaction is really quite fascinating. I will admit to you, since I have no background in economics whatsoever — I've always believed in [Pierre-Joseph] Proudhon's dictum that property is theft — but I'm gradually being converted, Hernando. But how does all of that, assuming that it is valid — and I don't dispute it for a moment — meet Dambisa's clarion call for jobs and Paul's recognition that Haiti is on the knife's edge, and that what must be done is infrastructure now in order to bring the private sector into the job creation business? We can forever discuss the undoubtedly fascinating and important dimensions which may come down the road. But how do you get the infrastructure now, if the only way you can get it is through public aid, and then open up the job markets through private capital? I think that's the essence of the argument.

RUDYARD GRIFFITHS: I'm going to ask Dambisa to end this question-and-answer session with a response to Stephen's remarks.

DAMBISA MOYO: Well, if it were so obvious that all we need to do is send money to get some infrastructure, then why haven't we done it after all this time?

STEPHEN LEWIS: Because it is Canada.

DAMBISA MOYO: I don't know if you're aware of this, but there have been some amazing innovations in Africa. The Pan African Infrastructure Development Fund [PAIDF] and the Development Bank of Southern Africa [DBSA] are two initiatives dedicated to raising private capital to finance infrastructure. Aside from the Chinese — and I entitle one of my chapters "The Chinese Are our Friends" — they are building infrastructure that the West has failed to build in sixty years. There are roads now in Africa, bridges, ports, railways, where there have not been for years.

If it is really just about infrastructure, then why don't you just go in and build the roads? What exactly is the problem? As far as I'm concerned, this is just sitting around and having a nice chat. We know what we can do. We know what has been done to generate growth and reduce poverty. There's no need to sit around here and start thinking about what it might be. Is it a matter of tribes? Is it a question of being landlocked? No. It is about jobs. You don't bring about those types of job-creating environments by relying on aid. We know what works. Let's implement it. Let's stop talking. The fact of the matter is we get an A for theory and an F for implementation. We know what works. Let's not forget that.

RUDYARD GRIFFITHS: We are going to have the final four-minute remarks from our speakers. We're going to do this in the opposite order that the introductory remarks were presented. So, Dambisa, we're going to give you the microphone first, followed by Paul, then Hernando, and then, Stephen, you'll conclude.

DAMBISA MOYO: I think I have already said most of what I wanted to say, but I do want to add a couple of things. It has been sixty years and a trillion dollars of aid. Let's not forget that. Peter Bauer, to whom my book is dedicated, was a Hungarian-born economist who was very critical of the aid system in the 1950s and 1960s. He was ostracized and pilloried and, honestly, if I had lived at that time as a policy-maker, I might have been one of the people throwing tomatoes at him. He came up with a brilliant quote, which I'll paraphrase here, that aid money is money taken from the poor in rich countries and sent to the rich in poor countries. I'm sad to say today that amongst a whole list of problems that Peter Bauer had anticipated, he was right. He died in 2002, and there was some semblance of him coming back into the fold, but he was essentially ignored.

There are two choices. You can side with Paul Collier and Stephen Lewis, who advocate the continuation of state models of aid, a continuation of taking money from developed nations and passing it along to the developing world. It is, by the way, no surprise that Hernando and I come from the emerging countries — the very places that you are trying to help — and we are telling you we don't want the money. On the other hand, you can vote for innovation, for a new approach — though it isn't really a new approach in the sense it is untried and untested. It is an approach that we know works. We know how to create jobs, we know how to put a man on the moon, we know how to get Africa out of the quagmire that it is currently in.

PAUL COLLIER: What would actually happen if the international community was not involved with Africa? We would be discussing China's involvement during this debate. I don't want to be too negative; China is doing some good things. But the idea that China would discipline African governments to provide property rights and good governance is hard to digest. Do you remember three or four years ago, the vice-president of China toured Africa and his calling card message was, "We don't ask any questions." What did he mean by that? In other words, an unrestrained China, without any international competition, would be a pretty dangerous thing. It would leave Africa in the cul-de-sac. Africa would go back to the model of resource extraction without benefit. Now, how do we get out of the cul-de-sac? And let's recognize that a cul-de-sac is what a lot of these countries are in. Dambisa says that we've had sixty years of aid and that it has been a failure, but actually, over those sixty years, aid has had periods of amazing success.

If we go back sixty years, which is when aid was invented, we see that it was invented in North America in order to restore my own region, Europe. Europe in the late 1940s was a fragile mess, both politically and economically. It was a ruin. And North America knew that it had to get serious, which is the difference between then and now. North America got serious by combining aid with intelligent trade policies, security policies, and efforts at governance. That worked. And then there was a period when aid, instead of being used to reconstruct societies, was used to buy Europe onto our side instead of the Soviet Union's side. Right through until the early 1990s, aid was diverted into a different agenda. Of course, it didn't develop Africa. It wasn't meant to. It was meant to buy the support of dictators. It doesn't have to be like that.

In a democracy, and the Organisation for Economic Co-operation and Development [OECD] countries that provide aid are all democracies, the quality of the policies depends on the citizens. In the past, most citizens from countries in the OECD have not been sufficiently engaged or sufficiently up to speed, so the aid policies have been put in place by politicians and have been gesture politics. It doesn't have to be like that. Citizens must get up to speed. That's the virtue of debates like this. Once you are informed, once there's a critical mass of informed citizens in Canada, in America, and in Europe, aid and the other array of development policies can become serious. We can repeat the success of sixty years ago when North America recovered Europe.

HERNANDO DE SOTO: We all care about development, each in our different way. I'm also glad that we have focused on Africa, having Dambisa Moyo, a brilliant author, as my debating mate. Africa is the continent that needs us the most. And it is good that we focused on it. That is why I'll point out again that the idea of the rule of law starts with property. You can't establish rule of law if you don't know who is where. It's as simple as that.

Because of the recession, we've lost focus on the fact that there is a food shortage in the world. And the food shortage is due to the fact that there are 1.7 billion hectares in the world that are being cultivated and that feed the whole globe. And it is obviously not enough. We have done the green revolution. We have done that, and we need more land. And there's 2.7 billion hectares left in the world, most of which are in Africa.

Unless you start giving indigenous Africans titles to their property, it will be taken over by the Chinese and by large corporations. Then you'll understand why it is so important to give property rights. The potential property owners may not have capital, but if they are given ownership, whoever is coming in to invest will say, "Well, you've got the land, but you can't do much with it unless I build a road. You can't do much unless I move the stones away. You can't do much unless I arrange the irrigation systems. I'll tell you what. I'll give you 50 percent." That's how capital begins. If you don't do that, Africa is up for grabs.

The next thing that I think is important to remember in all of this is that Canada is a great country because your two heads of Janus, facing opposite directions inside the country, have come to terms with each other. There are Canadians who believe in property rights and individual rights and growth, and in conquering the world, and in creating treasure and enterprise. And there are Canadians on the other side who like community, who want social harmony, who want to take care of the poor, who want to take care of women's rights, who want to take care of minorities. And the advantage in Canada is that your political system brings the two heads of Janus together. We have to find a way of structuring aid and communicating with developing countries in a coherent manner, instead of asking them to be victims of your right, through capitalist exploitation, or victims of your left, through fantasy projects.

And the important thing to understand with respect to indigenous people is that we will one day look left and right in Latin America, Africa, and Asia. That's the twenty-first century way to look at politics. But we're not there yet. Canada's indigenous people are not there. They are frozen in the 1876 *Indian Act*. The issue, when you're living in the nineteenth century, isn't left or right. It's up or down. Once you look at it that way, you can start talking.

STEPHEN LEWIS: I have three points to make, if I may. Let's provide a moment's perspective. I don't know where the trillion dollars comes from. I've never seen any precise sourcing —

DAMBISA MOYO: From the World Bank.

STEPHEN LEWIS: But this year, 35 billion dollars is going to Africa by way of foreign aid. You saw what we're paying for the General Motors bailout. It will be over 60 billion dollars. You saw what the Pentagon spends in a year. It's over 600 billion dollars. We now have 11.5 trillion dollars internationally devoted to bailouts and subsidies. What we're doing with Africa by way of aid, in response to requests, is so picayune and marginal that it shouldn't be overly inflated. It is an effort being made as genuinely as possible to provide the transition to fully vibrant and mixed economies. Number two, it's important and good to invite private capital in, but private capital tends to move to the one place where there is a predictable return, and that's in the natural resource sector. As a result China is developing oil in Sudan, and a number of private companies are in the Democratic Republic of Congo, which is having a war of the most insensate atrocity, which is rooted in the resource base. And it's important to recognize that private capital doesn't always go where you want it to go.

Yes, I'm preoccupied with sexual violence. It drives me crazy that a quarter of a million women have been raped in the Congo over the last several years, and it's running at a level of over a thousand a month in the Kivu alone — and it is all because of resources, and the resources are being developed by the private sector. It is terribly important to recognize that when one has these investments they don't always work quite as you would wish them to work. Witness Angola, as my colleague gave evidence for.

And the final point I want to make, which hasn't been introduced into this debate at all, is triggered by Hernando's reference to food. Two thousand of the world's most eminent scientists from the Intergovernmental Panel on Climate Change [IPCC] have come to the conclusion that the consequences of global warming — by the year 2030 —will be felt most forcefully in southern Africa. In other words, the consequences of global warming will impact all of the countries which are now consumed with the struggle against poverty and disease. Sometimes I think it's like some kind of conspiratorial network. But the fact of the matter is, if the panel is right — and so far we have underestimated the impact of climate change in the world — there will be more drought. There will be more famine. There will be more hunger. There will be an absence of household food and security. It is terribly important that the world need not be so self-centred.

And aid is just a vehicle to make humane and economically vibrant societies possible. It is not a mystery. It just works. It has been abused, but that's because of the way it was given. It need not be, and that's what we're arguing for.

SUMMARY: By evening's end, both sides had made such impassioned pleas that the audience vote barely changed. The pre-debate vote was 39 percent in favour of the resolution and 61 percent against. Post-debate the vote was 41 percent in favour and 59 percent against.

CLIMATE CHANGE

Be it resolved climate change is
mankind's defining crisis and demands
a commensurate response.

Pro: Elizabeth May and George Monbiot
Con: Lord Nigel Lawson and Bjørn Lomborg

December 1, 2009

CLIMATE CHANGE

INTRODUCTION: The Munk Debates tackled the highly charged matter of climate change shortly before the United Nations' historic Copenhagen Summit, which was held December 7–18, 2009. The debate also followed hard on the scandal involving the release of over 300 leaked emails and documents at the Climatic Research Unit and the University of East Anglia, which urged climate scientists to present a united front on global warming.

A holiday gift to attendees was the warmth provided by all the sparks flying as Canada's Elizabeth May, Leader of the Green Party, environmental lawyer, and activist; Sweden's Bjørn Lomborg, an environmentalist, adjunct professor at the Copenhagen Business School, and organizer of the Copenhagen Consensus Center; the U.K.'s Lord Nigel Lawson, a past Chancellor of the Exchequer and President of the British Institute of Energy Economics; and George Monbiot, an author and journalist, tackled the following resolution: Be it resolved climate change is mankind's defining crisis and commands a commensurate response.

Arguing the pro side were May and Monbiot, versus Lawson and Lomborg on the con side. While all the debaters agreed that CO_2 levels in the atmosphere were climbing steadily higher, bringing with them some challenges, differences arose when it came to how great a problem this was and whether or not some of the proposed cures were likely to cause more difficulties than they solved.

Lomborg and Lawson proposed that decarbonizing economies would make already low standards of living sink lower in the developing world. May and Monbiot saw a connection between virtually every problem faced in the developing world — famine, tribal wars, AIDS — and climate change. Monbiot, for example, suggested that AIDS was spread in Africa when drought brought about by climate change forced men to move from village to village. Lomborg noted that perhaps the use of condoms could help curb the spread of disease more efficiently and with fewer economic side effects than decarbonizing entire markets. This caused some laughter from the crowd but angered Elizabeth May.

LORD NIGEL LAWSON: Let me start by saying that I congratulate Peter and Melanie Munk and their foundation on holding this debate. Not least because this important issue — and I think we're all agreed on that — is seldom properly debated.

Believers in what to all intents and purposes has become a new secular religion — starting with former U.S. vice-president Al

Gore, who refuses to debate — constantly insist that dissent should be neither tolerated nor heard. And I hope that most of you here find that as disquieting as I do.

This debate is not about whether we care about the environment or not. We all care about the environment, and so we certainly should. No, this debate is about one very specific issue, which is whether to require policy decisions which I believe, if implemented, would be highly damaging. I interpret the motion as contending that prospective global warming is the most pressing issue facing humanity today, and that to avert it the world must decarbonize its economies in short order.

Now, the vast majority of climate scientists themselves don't believe the first part of this proposition. The most thorough survey of hundreds of accredited mainstream climate scientists was conducted a couple of years ago by Professor Hans von Storch of the Meteorological Institute of the University of Hamburg. And it asked a considerable number of questions, one of which is highly relevant to our debate. And it was, "What is the most pressing issue facing humanity today?" How many of the climate scientists do you think answered either "climate change" or "global warming"? Just 8 percent gave that answer. Only 8 percent thought that climate change or global warming was the biggest issue facing humanity today. And when you look into the issue, that derisory figure becomes thoroughly understandable.

As most of you know, the Intergovernmental Panel on Climate Change [IPCC] is the body that the world's governments principally rely upon for their analyses. And in its most recent report, the IPCC calculated the likely cost of climate change based on elaborate computer models. Incidentally, those models projected a marked acceleration of global warming during this century following the very modest recorded warming in the last quarter of the twentieth century, and in fact, so far this century, there has been no further recorded global warming.

Moreover, the single most important source for the IPCC's global temperature series is the small group of scientists at the Climatic Research Unit [CRU] in the U.K.[2] Recent leaked emails have revealed serious incompetence and apparent skullduggery there, and I have called for a full and thorough inquiry.

I would like to take this moment to salute George Monbiot, whose views I don't share, but whom I recognize as a man of integrity, who has gone even further and publicly demanded the resignation of the head of the CRU.

To return to the IPCC report, let us, to be on the safe side, take the upper end of the IPCC's projected temperature range for the year 2100 — the upper end of its estimate of the cost of that warming, and the gloomiest of its six economic scenarios. And let us further assume that the relative cost of this warming for the developing world will be twice that for the world as a whole.

It's not difficult to calculate, as I do in my book [*An Appeal to Reason: A Cool Look at Global Warming*] — and that calculation has never been questioned — what this would mean for living standards in the developing world. The answer is this: in a hundred years' time, average living standards in the

---

[2] The Climatic Research Unit, founded in 1972, is part of the School of Environmental Sciences at the University of East Anglia in Norwich, England.

developing world, instead of being nine and a half times as high as they are today, would be only eight and a half times as high as they are today. So is this man's defining crisis, the most pressing issue facing humanity today? If only.

As for the second part of the motion, the so-called commensurate response of drastically decarbonizing the global economy, it can readily be shown that the cost of doing this would far exceed any benefits it could conceivably bring. Moreover — and this matters a great deal — there is an even more important moral dimension. The reason we use carbon-based energy is simply that it is far and away the cheapest large-scale source of energy, and is likely to remain so for the foreseeable future.

Switching to much more expensive energy may be acceptable to us in the developed world, but in the developing world there are still tens if not hundreds of millions of people suffering from desperate poverty, and from the consequences of that poverty in the shape of malnutrition, preventable disease, and premature death.

So for the developing world, the overriding priority has to be the fastest feasible rate of economic growth, which, among other things, means relying on the cheapest available source of energy, which is carbon-based energy. To deny them this would be positively obscene. Which is why, of course, there will be no Kyoto-style agreement at the 2009 United Nations Climate Change Conference in Copenhagen.

But there still remains the ugly spectre of protectionism. The cap and trade bill, the American Clean Energy and Security Act of 2009 [ACES] that is currently stalled in the U.S. Congress, contains a provision to impose punitive tariffs on imports from countries like India and China, which are not prepared to forswear cheap energy. And France has urged the European Union to follow suit. At a time then when we are trying to emerge from the worst world recession since the 1930s, that really is all we need. This policy is madness.

So, in conclusion, what then? Throughout the millennia that we've been around, mankind has successfully adapted to the changing climate that nature has provided, just as we adapt today to the very different climates that exist in different parts of the world. And, aided by more and more advanced technology than we've ever had at our disposal, that is what we should continue to do. The motion before us is scientifically unfounded, economically damaging, and profoundly immoral. And that is why I invite you to reject it.

RUDYARD GRIFFITHS: Elizabeth, please present your opening arguments.

ELIZABETH MAY: I'm very pleased to be here and quite honoured, and I want to thank the Aurea Foundation. And I want to say, with all due respect, that the people here are not the experts. You have before you me, a lawyer who became a politician; Lord Lawson, a journalist who became a politician; Bjørn Lomborg, a statistician who became a best-selling author, and a wonderful *Guardian* journalist, George Monbiot.

The real experts on this subject who matter are the scientists on the IPCC, and policy experts around the world. So with all due respect to this debate, I also wish to say that I am grieved that in the year 2009, we're asking the question, "Should we act in response to the climate crisis, is it a defining issue for humanity?" I would have wished that seven days before the opening of the Copenhagen meetings, which is the fifteenth Conference of the Parties to the United Nations Framework Convention on Climate Change, we would have accepted what most of the knowledgeable scientists around the globe see as our top threat, the climate crisis, followed very closely by the water crisis, which will be exacerbated by ignoring climate.

So what have we learned and what did we know, and why do I say that it is a shame that we are debating this issue? Well, we should ask, if we could have rewritten this question, "How do we reach the targets that have been set for us by a scientific community that wants to warn us and avert catastrophe?" Not "if" we should do it.

I want to take you back to a conference that took place in Toronto in the last week of June 1988. I'm drawn to that as a starting point because, as Canadians, some of us forget that we were ever in the lead on this issue. But we were in those days. And we were the sponsors, along with the United Nations' agencies, of the first international large scientific comprehensive public gathering to examine the climate crisis. It was called the World Conference on the Changing Atmosphere: Implications for Global Security. And a consensus statement from that conference began with this sentence — and I think it answers the question we are examining during this debate: "Humanity is conducting an unintended, uncontrolled, globally pervasive experiment, whose ultimate consequences could be second only to global nuclear war."

The science since 1988, despite anything you may have heard, has only gotten stronger. The evidence that has been put together by the IPCC was covered in that year by governments recognizing that not every politician has been a scientist and is able to absorb the data. Although I'd like to give credit to the former Prime Minister of the United Kingdom, Margaret Thatcher, who described herself as a scientist who became a politician and who said in 1990, at the end of the second world climate conference: "The threat to our world comes not only from tyrants and their tanks. It can be more insidious and less visible. The danger of global warming is as yet unseen, but real enough for us to make changes and sacrifices so that we do not live at the expense of future generations."

What does the science of climate change tell us? It tells us, incontrovertibly, the following things. Humanity has already changed the chemistry of our atmosphere. Through the profligate burning of fossil fuels, we have released so much carbon dioxide into the atmosphere that we have literally changed the chemistry of the atmosphere to the point that this year there is 30 percent more carbon dioxide in our atmosphere, more than at any time in the last million years.

Now, how could we possibly know that? We know that because of some of the most sophisticated science that has ever taken place, twenty-first-century science, examining Antarctic ice core data. We know when the ice was formed, and every piece of ice can be dated. And ice never freezes completely solid. So there are air bubbles, and every air bubble is like a time capsule into the atmosphere, and the chemistry of our atmosphere when that ice was formed.

We know that carbon dioxide is a powerful warming gas, and that without the natural greenhouse effect this planet would be too cold to sustain life. So we know we're conducting a vast experiment on very large climate systems over which we'll have very little control if we don't reduce fossil fuel use quickly and protect forests and expand them. The science on the climate issue was established in terms of its essentials quite a long time ago. Where the uncertainties were was whether climate change had already started.

Are we seeing observed levels of climate change that rise above the noise of regular climate variation? And yes, 2005 tied with 1998 as the hottest year on record. But we're looking at a system with enormous time lags. It's not about year on year temperature change. These changes are seen in decades, and in those terms it is clear that the trend continues.

That's why the scientists around the world, and that's why the governments around the world, are not troubled by something I'm sure our opposing team members will want to make much of during this debate. But the East Anglia university centre was doing one small piece of the work. I've brought with me tonight — and I've read all the thousands of emails that were illegally hacked from the university centre's computer. And when you read all the thousands of emails that were illegally hacked from the university centre's computer and the whole train of that information, it is very clear there was no dishonesty there. They are decent scientists trying to do their work, and finding they are increasingly unable to do the research they want to do because they are so troubled and harassed, because they have been ensnared in something political. They are honest scientists, but even so their work is only one strand.

The redundancy of the evidence and the observed effects is overwhelming — millions of square kilometres of ice are gone much faster than the IPCC projected. We're seeing dramatic changes around the world. We see them in the retreating glaciers, we see them in the rising sea levels — sea levels have risen 80 percent faster than the third IPCC report projected.

These are the observed effects that match with the theory that match with the evidence that when you throw increasing warming gases into a planet's atmosphere, you can expect very large and dangerous changes. We know enough to know that we need to act, and that's why governments around the world signed and ratified the Framework Convention on Climate Change in 1992.

Since that time, political will has failed to deliver. Some countries have succeeded — and it's to their credit. But seven days away from the Climate Change Conference in Copenhagen, now is the time for citizens around the world to double the resolve to speak loudly and clearly to their political leaders and tell them to abide by the warnings of scientists who have made it abundantly clear we have run down the clock, we have run out of all of our time for delay, denial, and procrastination. In the interest of the security of our civilization, our economy, our society, and future generations, this time we have to act.

BJØRN LOMBORG: It's a pleasure to be here and it's an important discussion. Human nature is a funny thing. We don't seem to be able to take anything seriously unless we add a superlative. It is not enough that things are good; they have to be the best. Or, if it is going to be bad, it has to be really, really bad. It has to be the worst thing ever.

We are being asked during this debate, "Is this the defining crisis for mankind?" Elizabeth was trying to downplay it a little bit, but she also said that it is the top priority. And, of course, that matters. If it were just "Is this an important issue?" I think we would all agree and we could go home. The question is — is this the most important thing?

This escalation of rhetoric is not just stylistic. It forces us back to the very essence of a dichotomy. You're either for us or you're against us. You either believe that global warming is the worst thing ever to befall mankind or you're an enemy of humankind. I think this kind of approach is fundamentally unsound. And it actually is a poor way of both helping the world and dealing with global warming.

Let me elaborate on that. First of all, is global warming really mankind's defining crisis? There are 3 billion people who live in extreme poverty. There are 2.4 billion people who don't have access to clean energy. There are a billion people who will go to bed hungry. There are 3 billion people who don't have access to clean drinking water and sanitation. In the year 2009, 15 million people — a quarter of everyone who dies in this world — will die from easily curable infectious diseases. Is global warming really the only, and top, priority? I don't think so.

We've asked some of the world's leading economists — the Copenhagen Consensus — how can you actually do the most good for the world? These economists looked at all the different problems in the world and told us where we could do the most good.

They told us it was about investing in ending malnutrition. They told us it was about investing in agriculture and research and development, and immunization of easily curable infectious diseases, and it was about the education of girls. This is all pretty boring stuff. But it's incredibly important to make sure that we live in a better world.

And saying that global warming is the defining crisis of mankind cheapens all these other problems. But that doesn't mean we shouldn't try to tackle climate change. Of course we should. Climate change is real. It is a big problem. But I would also argue that putting so much focus on global warming and claiming that it is the defining issue of mankind neglects that we need to be smarter about global warming.

Elizabeth said, in a somewhat offended manner, that we have listened to all the evidence from the scientists for so long but we don't have the political will to actually carry through. That's true. But maybe we should then start thinking that this is because we're barking up the wrong tree. Maybe it is because we're approaching climate change in the wrong way. And as long as we do that we're going to say, let's throw everything overboard and focus on this. Let's cut carbon emissions dramatically in the rich world, right now. But the costs are phenomenal. Economists tell us the costs of doing that, to keep to the two degrees centigrade limit that many nations have signed on to, will cost, by the end of the century, some 40 trillion dollars a year. That is 40 trillion dollars. The net benefit will be to avoid climate damages of about 3 trillion dollars. We are buying a cure that's much more costly than the ailment.

Of course we're having a hard time getting nations on board. That is because we are saying that this is the worst crisis mankind has ever faced. We've got to dial it back.

And the economists surveyed in the Copenhagen Consensus told us that it is about investing in research and development and investing in green energy technology. It is about making sure that future technology becomes so cheap that everybody will want to buy it. We might put up solar panels for now. Rich, well-meaning people will put them up, to show what good people they are. But fundamentally, that is not going to make a difference where global warming is concerned. Only once we have made sure that solar panels and all the other technologies are so cheap that we can get everybody to buy them — the Chinese and the Indians — only then will we have solved the problem of global warming.

I would argue because we are so singularly focused on global warming, we forget about all the other problems in this world. And because we are so singularly focused on this being the most important problem, we end up making poor policy decisions.

So I would agree with Elizabeth. We do need a different approach. We need to stop talking about cutting carbon emissions, cutting this, cutting that. We have done that. For twenty years, we have done that. We promised cuts at the United Nations Conference on Environment and Development [UNCED] in Rio in 1992, and we didn't deliver. We promised cuts during the United Nations Framework Convention on Climate Change in Kyoto in 1997, and we didn't deliver. We promised further cuts and we didn't deliver. And now we're going to the United Nations Climate Change Conference in Copenhagen and promising even grander gestures.

If this is going to be anything more than just another conference with confetti and champagne — if we're going to do something other than waste another ten years not doing anything about global warming — then we've got to start being smart.

Global warming is a big problem. It's definitely one of the things we need to fix in the twenty-first century. But we have many problems to fix. We need to fix global warming with intelligence. So I would suggest that you should vote "no" to this resolution, not because you don't want to do good, but exactly because you want to do the most good possible. You want to recognize that we should deal with climate change, but you want to recognize that it should be dealt with smartly. And you want to recognize that global warming, while important, is by no means the only challenge we face this century. I ask you to vote "no" to this resolution.

GEORGE MONBIOT: Hidden in the motion before you is a question. How lucky do you feel? Lord Nigel Lawson and Bjørn Lomborg tell us that we should feel very lucky indeed. What they are telling us is that we should prepare not for the worst case scenario, not for the middle case scenario, not even for the best case scenario, but for the better than best case scenario.

That is because the projections and the costs of climate change they are talking about are more optimistic than the most optimistic end of the spectrum in all the major reports.

Lord Nigel Lawson tells us that so flawed and unsatisfactory is climate science that despite everything we know, there has been no further warming this century. I congratulate him. He has single-handedly beat those scientists at their little game, exposed their dastardly plans, and demonstrated that the entire temperature series produced by all the monitoring stations around the world must be wrong, because what they tell us is that eight out of the ten warmest years ever recorded have taken place since 2001. How lucky do you feel?

Bjørn takes a different tack and says that, yes, climate change is real. He doesn't go in for this stuff about it being a great conspiracy, or that warming isn't happening and that all the climate scientists have got it wrong. What he tells us is that, actually, the costs of living with climate change are very low, and the costs of trying to prevent runaway climate change are very high. Well, this is exactly the opposite conclusion to the one reached by the most thorough scholarly and lengthy review into the economic costs of climate change, the Stern Review on the Economics of Climate Change, commissioned by the U.K. government and headed up by economist Lord Nicholas Stern and his vast team. They proposed that the costs of preventing high levels of climate change were roughly 1 percent of the gross domestic product [GDP] — which sounds quite a lot.

But the costs of trying to live with those levels of climate change, at the very best case, amounted to 5 percent of GDP, and at the worst case amounted to 20 percent of GDP. So who do you believe? Do you believe Bjørn Lomborg or do you believe the Stern Review? How lucky do you feel?

Both men have talked breezily about adaptation. We can adapt to climate change. Whatever it throws at us, we are ingenious, remarkable apes who can sort out solutions to these troubles. Yes, I believe that in the rich world we can probably get along with two or three degrees of climate change — for a few decades, at any rate — and we can potentially adapt to it. But it's a very different story in the parts of the poor world with which I am familiar.

We hear that adaptation technologies can be used to ensure that the crisis can be staved off. Drip irrigation, new crop varieties, air conditioning — it sounds all very orderly and very sensible. But in the real world that's not how it works.

I worked for a long time in the Horn of Africa, the region that includes the countries of Eritrea, Djibouti, Ethopia, and Somalia, and I saw the first of the great climate change droughts which have stricken that region, hitting it again and again. These are droughts of the scale and severity that they once experienced every forty or fifty years, but have been happening every two or three years recently.

You've probably been seeing horrendous pictures of what has been happening to the Turkana people of northwest Kenya, hit by droughts which even in their oral traditions — which go back a long way — are unprecedented. What is the adaptation technology of choice there? It's not drip irrigation. It's the AK-47. As soon as a severe drought hits, the killing begins. Bjørn presents us with a choice of investing in foreign aid and helping the world's people to avoid poverty, famine, malaria, and other diseases, or investing in preventing climate change.

But why should the money for preventing climate change come out of the foreign aid budget? Is that a major part of government spending? It is far from it. Foreign aid is a tiny part of government spending. Why shouldn't it come out of the military budget for invading Iraq? Or the tens of billions of dollars used to subsidize the oil and gas industries, or the completely unnecessary subsidies for the agricultural industry? The answer to the question of whether we should invest in foreign aid or whether we should invest in climate change prevention is "yes, we should invest in climate change prevention."

This is the time to face the greatest threat I believe humanity has faced, without which we cannot tackle any of the other problems that Bjørn has so rightly highlighted, and that all of us are concerned about. The conference in Copenhagen is, I believe, a historic moment for humankind.

And the question before the members at the Copenhagen Climate Conference and the question before us during this debate is this. It's very simple. Do we carry on as we are, dumping our costs on people who are not responsible for climate change but who must carry those costs? Or do we pick up our responsibility, do we recognize the scale of this huge defining crisis, and do we produce a response commensurate with that crisis? How lucky do you feel?

RUDYARD GRIFFITHS: I want to allow each of you to rebut each other in terms of what you've heard. Nigel, since you spoke first, I'd like you to start. What have you heard that you fundamentally disagree with?

LORD NIGEL LAWSON: Well, a great deal — pretty well everything on the other side. I will focus first on two issues which are so clear that they shouldn't require long elaboration.

George Monbiot is quite incapable of understanding the difference between a level and a trend. I will explain with a simple example. Supposing a country's population had been rising and rising and rising, and then it stopped rising. The population flattened out. Then, it would be absolutely true that the population had stopped rising. This is a very significant point, and this is what has happened with recorded temperatures during this century.

It would also be true, of course, to say that the population was at the highest it had been for a long time, because it had flattened out at the level it had reached before. So George is absolutely wrong to say that there is no proof of this. Many scientists — he's not a scientist, so perhaps he doesn't know — admit that there has been no recorded global warming so far this century. Anybody who denies that really doesn't know what they're talking about.

That is a fact, and it has been revealed in the emails from the CRU. They say it is a travesty that there is no explanation for this unexpected development. That's in the email traffic. This is very embarrassing for us, they say.

The other thing George Monbiot said is that the great authority on this matter is the Stern Review, and the Stern Review said that to fix this would only cost 1 percent of GDP.

First of all, only a few months after Stern had written that in the review — or his team had written it — he said, oh, by the way, I made a mistake. It's not 1 percent, it's 2 percent.

And that was actually reported in the *Guardian*, and quite prominently. But it wasn't reported in George's column.

Second, the Stern Review is disregarded by every serious economist who has addressed it. Dieter Helm, Official Fellow in Economics at Oxford, who is concerned about climate change, says that the figures are assumed figures. He gives them no credence at all —things will be much more expensive, he says. William D. Nordhaus, Sterling Professor of Economics at Yale University, says the figures contained in the Stern Review are absurd. Professor Martin Weitzman at Harvard University Department of Economics says the same. Professor Sir Partha Dasgupta, Frank Ramsey Professor at Economics at the University of Cambridge, says the same. Richard S. J. Tol, Professor of Economics at the Vrije Universiteit, Amsterdam, who is probably the economist who has studied this matter most extensively, says that the figures in the Stern Review are absolute — he uses a more polite word, but I will summarize it — rubbish.

This is not surprising because there are two things you should know about the Stern Review. First of all, Nicholas Stern was a government employee who was asked by the government to produce a justification for the policies that had already been announced and adopted. Secondly, the Stern Review has never been peer-reviewed. And indeed, it is unlikely it would do very well if it were.

RUDYARD GRIFFITHS: Elizabeth, I want you to answer the question, is the world getting warmer or not? And, George, maybe you can talk about the Stern Review.

ELIZABETH MAY: Well, in terms of the warmest years on record, it is a mug's game for many scientists.

They don't like to focus on individual years. It's very clear from the IPCC that anyone who understands atmospheric chemistry and atmospheric science and climate science knows that we are dealing with very large systems. And land mass does tend to warm up faster than water. So the land mass is warming at a different rate from the oceans; the oceans are the vast volume and surface area of this planet.

By the way, neither Bjørn Lomborg nor Lord Lawson is going to want to tell you what happens with carbon dioxide in our atmosphere: it acidifies our oceans and threatens life there. Perhaps we can touch on that later, because they don't bother to talk about it in either of their books.

So what do we know about what is happening to global average temperature? Decade on decade, which is what you'd expect to see in terms of timelines, you see increasing warming. In terms of this century, there is a difference. And because Lord Lawson mentioned that we can read it in the emails, I grabbed one of them. I have them all with me and I took the trouble, before wondering whether there was some scandal lurking in what they call "Climategate," the Climatic Research Unit email controversy, to read all of the emails.

And there is a similarity between Climategate and the Watergate scandal. And it is this: what was stolen is immaterial. The question is, who were the burglars and who paid them? I'd like to know who breaks into university computers and hacks into emails.

Here's one of the emails, just for fun, discussing the temperature data year on year, and this is a scientist at NASA communicating with a scientist at the University of East Anglia. And they are saying that, yes, we do have a discrepancy. The Met Office Hadley Centre for Climate Change has got different data than NASA, which reports that 2005 was the warmest year on record and that 2007 tied with 1998 for second place. The Hadley Centre, which was created by former Prime Minister Margaret Thatcher so that the U.K. would have a good meteorological service looking at climate, is showing temperature decreases after 1998.

The scientists in these emails are speculating that the difference is due to the fact that the Hadley Centre data doesn't contain as much information from the Arctic. So if you happen to be someone who is reading the private emails of these climate scientists, you can find that on October 8, 2008, 1:50 p.m., an email that was part of this back and forth between scientists makes it clear that the Hadley Centre doesn't have the same data that NASA has.

The NASA scientists are very clearly saying that 2005 was the warmest year on record, at least tied with 1998. And I've checked with the IPCC scientists in Canada, who are the authorities who should be talking to you about this. I'm talking about people like Richard Peltier, a physicist at the University of Toronto; Gordon McBean, a climatologist at the University of Western Ontario, and Andrew J. Weaver, a climate scientist at the School of Earth and Ocean Sciences at the University of Victoria, all people who could probably explain this much better than I can.

But there's no question that the warming trend continues,

decade on decade. But more importantly than temperature, we have issues of chemistry and the phenomenon of
increased CO_2 levels, up to 387 parts per million, when at no
time in the million years before the Industrial Revolution did
it ever exceed 280 parts per million.

RUDYARD GRIFFITHS: George, did Stern pick the most extreme
scenario, the most extreme outcome, in order to gauge public policy, or did he provide a mainstream analysis of the
challenge?

GEORGE MONBIOT: Well, having accused the world's scientists of effectively making up their temperature record,
Nigel Lawson then goes on to accuse the British government of trying to commit economic suicide. Because what
he is effectively saying is that the government asked Stern
to come up with the most extreme scenario, to justify
spending as much money as possible in averting climate
change.

What the government asked Stern to do was to find out
how much it would cost so that it could adjust its policies
accordingly. And it did so. And the Stern Review indicated
that the costs were far greater than the government had
anticipated. Stern didn't follow government policy. The
result of the Review was bad news that the government
didn't want to hear — that climate change would cost a lot
more than was previously anticipated.

Was it an extreme scenario? No. It was the most scholarly
and thorough review ever conducted, and far from being not
peer-reviewed, it was the great review of reviews. This is

about as high as it goes, as far as reviewing is concerned. It reviewed the peer-reviewed literature to come up with an über-review, a meta-review, of what was going on. That's what the Stern Review is all about.

And I just want very briefly to touch on this temperature issue. Eight of the ten warmest years on record happened in this century. And the question I want to ask is directed to Bjørn. What do you make of Nigel Lawson's contention that there has been no further warming this century?

BJØRN LOMBORG: Two things. I will get back to answering your question, but first, let's just remember the Stern Review, because this is actually important, and I think the point that Elizabeth May made, that we need to listen to scientists, is correct. Of course we do.

I think all of us here have listened to scientists and said, yes, global warming is real and it is an important problem. But we also need to listen to economists, who tell us that we should handle this problem smartly, rather than stupidly.

The problem is that the Stern Review is an extreme example. It is almost universally disparaged by economists. Professor Richard Tol actually did a survey of the implicit carbon price, which is a way of asking, how extreme is it? The Stern Review is in the 97th percentile. It's not a mainstream review.

And just for your edification, you might want to know that *Nature* magazine uncovered that before the British government asked Stern, they also asked two other people to work on this review and let those people know, very specifically, that what should come out of this review was a supporting argument for the British government's policies. And these two people said no.

Now there's no doubt — and I've talked to Stern many times — that he sincerely and honestly believed what he wrote, so he was not being dishonest. But it was very clear that he was asked to do this.

And it's also very important, as George Monbiot rightly mentioned, to remember that this was a review of other people's research. Stern didn't do any research of his own. If you compare the numbers, of all the numbers that he put into the model, they indicate that the damages from climate change range from -1 percent — and that is actually a benefit from global warming — to a damage of 4 percent. The most likely outcome is a damage of about 2 percent. That was something that Nicholas Stern massaged into a number of 5 to 20 percent. It's simply not credible.

Let's just remember, if this were George Monbiot looking at us talking about climate science, he would say that there were thousands of scientists that agree with these numbers. And then he would say that you cannot pick only one other scientist who says global warming isn't true. And I would absolutely agree with that.

But likewise, of course, you can't mention one economist that happened to be picked out for a very specific political reason, an economist who came up with a totally unjustifiable report, and say, "That's the report that I am going to look at. That report gives me the right numbers." You cannot do that when all the other climate economists tell us that what is prescribed in the Stern Review represents a very, very poor way to deal with the problem.

Yes, climate science is important, let's listen to the large majority of climate scientists telling us global warming is real. But let's also listen to the vast number of climate economists telling us that the proposed solutions we hear from very many scientists are simply rubbish.

RUDYARD GRIFFITHS: My next question is to Nigel Lawson. We have dental insurance, car insurance, home insurance — in other words, we take a portion of our incomes each year to mitigate risk in our lives. So how do you address the argument coming out of the Stern Review, which is that it is 1 or 2 percent of GDP, but we're insuring ourselves against a worst case scenario? Why do you think that this is an argument by which we shouldn't necessarily be captivated?

LORD NIGEL LAWSON: Well, climate change isn't a case of insurance, technically. Insurance is a statistically assessed risk, and if the risk eventuates — like the house burning down — you are compensated for the cost of the house burning down. There's no question of compensation here. This is like making the house thoroughly fireproof for a cost that is more than the house is worth. And that is not a sensible thing to do.

The figures that I was using — and remember, I took a worst case scenario from the IPCC range, which I think they may well exaggerate — are the figures which show that the living standards in the developing world, instead of being nine and a half times what they are today, will only be eight and a half times what they are today.

And that is not the biggest catastrophe — I don't want that to happen, I'd like living standards to be nine and a half times, or even better — but that is not the biggest catastrophe that could impact the planet. Nor is it right to expect countries in the developing world to condemn millions of people to unnecessary death, which is what going to more expensive energy implies, simply because it will make you feel good.

RUDYARD GRIFFITHS: Let me go to you, Elizabeth, because I think that's on many people's minds. Mitigating climate probably means not doing many other things. There are cost trade-offs in what you're proposing. We live in a world of finite budgets, we have a finite global economy. So how do you respond to the charge that aggressive action on climate change could lead to less support for all those essential human needs in the developing world?

ELIZABETH MAY: Well, I wish there was someone here from the developing world to make this point very clearly. A lot of people in the developing world are very concerned about the impact of the climate crisis, which as George Monbiot has already pointed out has caused extreme drought and extreme difficulties around the world.

The reality of it is that we might have believed it was hard to find money and that there were competing trade-offs, before we just went through a year in which four trillion dollars went to bailing out the financial system in the U.S. And I don't remember any economist — Bjørn, you never thrust yourself in front of the moving economic stimulus package juggernaut to say, "Wait, is that the best choice? We have competing values!" Bjørn functions as a propagandist to stop action on the climate crisis.

BJØRN LOMBORG: Elizabeth, if you're going to make that claim, you have to be honest and say, this is not about saying, should we do all the good things for the Third World and —

ELIZABETH MAY: I've been very honest, Bjørn, but you are someone who has broken integrity.

BJØRN LOMBORG: We spend 90, 95, 98 percent of our money on ourselves. Obviously, money would be much better spent on the Third World for hospitals and everything else. I'm simply asking about the money that we do spend on the Third World. Should we spend it well, or poorly?

ELIZABETH MAY: You seem to throw yourself in front of stopping action on the climate crisis, when other money is being spent. Where are you and your Copenhagen Consensus? Let me just make clear, last night I happened to be talking with a minister for poverty alleviation from the government of Lesotho. It was during an event in Ottawa with King Letsie III of Lesotho, where a lot of us work on actually trying to help this country in Africa, which has the third highest rate of HIV/AIDS in the world with 40 percent of its children orphaned.

And I put to the minister that I would be debating someone from Denmark who wanted to make the claim that it would be wrong to spend too much averting the climate crisis, because we should put our money into poverty alleviation and fighting HIV/AIDS instead.

And he said — and I must say, he was enraged: "But the climate crisis is making HIV/AIDS worse in my country every day." He said, "We are suffering" —

BJØRN LOMBORG: How is that possible, Elizabeth?

ELIZABETH MAY: "We cannot grow our food," the minister for poverty alleviation in Lesotho told me last night!

RUDYARD GRIFFITHS: Let's hear George Monbiot talk about the trade-offs between spending money now to cope with foreign aid versus the long-term challenge of global warming.

GEORGE MONBIOT: The first thing to bear in mind is that very little is spent on foreign aid. I would love to see us spend a lot more. And I don't know a single climate change activist who isn't also concerned about poverty, who isn't also concerned about disease, who isn't also concerned about hunger. In fact, that's why we're climate change activists. Climate change exacerbates all of those problems. You laugh at Elizabeth's example about AIDS, but I heard someone from Oxfam recently explaining exactly how it works, and they were talking about Malawi. They said climate change causes drought, and the drought forces the men off the land, as they have to go and find work elsewhere. So they leave the land, they leave their villages, they find work elsewhere, and of course they meet prostitutes, and then they bring AIDS back to their communities. So it might sound like an implausible and crazy suggestion, but according to Oxfam, it's quite true.

Now, we're presented with this choice over costs: if, on the one hand, we spend nothing and carry on as we are, and on the other hand we spend a lot of money and potentially bankrupt ourselves in doing so.

But if you read the latest *World Energy Outlook* by the International Energy Agency [IEA], published in November 2009, it says that in order to maintain global energy supplies, not using some sort of wacky transition of any kind at all, just carrying on the way we are, between now and 2030, we need to spend 25.6 trillion U.S. dollars.

The report says that because of the concentration of oil reserves in the Organization of the Petroleum Exporting Countries [OPEC], the net transfer of wealth from the non-OPEC nations to the OPEC nations, between now and 2030, will be a further 30 trillion U.S. dollars.

This isn't a choice between carrying on as we are and dancing through the buttercups and watching the bunnies hopping around and not spending anything, or splashing out huge amounts of money on alternative energy. Either way, if we're going to maintain energy supplies, we have to spend a huge amount of money.

And bear in mind that the IEA figures assume that those energy supplies hold up, and that the price of oil does not peak during that period. If oil does peak, those costs will go through the roof. The 150 dollars a barrel that we saw last year would be nothing by comparison to the cost of oil.

And there are a lot of other reasons why, for our economic well-being, we should cast aside our dependency on fossil fuels as quickly as we can.

RUDYARD GRIFFITHS: I would like to ask Nigel Lawson if you disagree with the worst case scenarios. Do you feel that there are secondary effects that could be quite positive as a result of the defossilization of our economy? Let's say, more energy independence. Let's say, less conflict affecting a world where our economy is quite fragile and depends on globalization. Do you sense that those kinds of secondary effects could be valuable?

LORD NIGEL LAWSON: No, I don't think so at all. I'm in favour of research and development in science and technology. You never know what you might discover. You might discover things that are extremely useful to mankind.

Take the peak oil point. I was Secretary for Energy in the United Kingdom in 1981, a long time ago. And I was told then that we had only forty years left of oil in the world. Fast-forward to the present, what are we told? We've got only forty years of oil left in the world. In fact, there's an enormous amount of oil. There have been big finds recently, in Iran and off the Gulf of Mexico.

Indeed, there is a sort of curious mismatch, because if oil were really running out there wouldn't be this huge attempt by oil companies to find new oil all over the world. Also, the technology of getting oil from shale is particularly interesting in the Canadian context. There have been big breakthroughs there.

China is not going to move to expensive energy, so the idea of the global agreement to cut back on carbon dioxide is not going to happen. As Bjørn says, we have to look at a different approach to this.

And what is China doing now? China is the new imperial power in Africa. China is dominating sub-Saharan Africa. It is buying out raw material resources of all kinds throughout sub-Saharan Africa. And that includes oil. It is now getting a big stake in Nigerian oil, in Angolan oil, and in Ghanaian oil. They would not be doing this if they didn't intend to use the oil. And they will be using the oil.

RUDYARD GRIFFITHS: Bjørn, I'm going to go to you and then to Elizabeth. Further to George and Elizabeth's point, about rising CO_2 levels in the atmosphere, if we're on to 450 parts per million, 500 parts per million, what is the tipping point for you? What is the moment where you get genuinely worried?

BJØRN LOMBORG: I'll talk about that and one other thing. I think, fundamentally, yes, we are going to see dramatic increases in CO_2 emissions. And George and Elizabeth would probably accept that, yes, China is going to be hard to rein in.

China just promised, in this fantasy game in Copenhagen, that they were going to cut their carbon intensity — that is, how much carbon they put out for every dollar they produce — somewhere between 40 and 45 percent by 2020. And people were immediately saying, the U.S. is only planning to cut 3 percent, but China is doing 40 percent. Of course, these are very different things.

If you take the IEA predictions for 2020, they show that if China did nothing whatsoever — because they're going to move towards producing more services and technology rather than steel and cement — they will improve their carbon ration dramatically. We expect them, without doing anything at all, to reduce their carbon intensity by 40 percent.

So they actually came out and said, we solemnly pledge to do nothing at all. But everybody loved them for it! The point here is that we will see a dramatic increase in emissions even though we are all going to get much more efficient.

The only way we can do something about this problem is by having better technology. We cannot ask developing countries — we can't even ask developed nations — to cut back on their carbon emissions. But if we have better technology, we will be able to do so simply because it will be cheaper for us to do so.

I would also very much like to point out that George Monbiot says that everyone he knows thinks we should focus more on doing something about poverty alleviation, about hunger, about all these other problems. George has just moved over to our side, admitting that climate change is not the defining crisis. It is one of the many crises we face in the twenty-first century. So thanks, George, for moving over here.

But moreover, look at what Elizabeth said — I think she probably regrets it a little — we should do something about global warming because of AIDS.

ELIZABETH MAY: I don't regret it because it's true.

BJØRN LOMBORG: George also made that point. It probably is

true that there are connections everywhere. You could probably make the argument that droughts and other things that come from global warming will exacerbate HIV/AIDS. But is that really the way we want to help people with HIV/AIDS? To say, let's cut back on carbon emissions so that in a hundred years the AIDS problem will be slightly less worse by the end of the century instead of, I don't know, handing out condoms?

The fundamental point is, do you want to be remembered for doing very little at a very high cost, or do you want to be remembered for having done a lot?

RUDYARD GRIFFITHS: Elizabeth, let's bring you back into this. I think the question on some people's minds is whether the pro side are being selective about your embrace of science and technology. What about the ability of technology to ameliorate emissions through innovation, through new kinds of energy production and distribution? Are you pessimistic about technology?

ELIZABETH MAY: Absolutely not. That's the problem with debating someone like Bjørn. He puts forward straw men and false choices, but whoever said that people who want action on climate change were against efficient technologies? We're the ones calling for the things that have already been invented. We have really important innovations that we could list, but it would take too long because there are hundreds of them.

The thing that is keeping them from completely taking over the marketplace, so that fossil fuels disappear, is that we haven't priced carbon. But when we stop burning oil in our cars, we'll also be removing a lot of the precursors to smog, increasing health and well-being. We're leaving out all of the benefits of taking action on climate change during this debate. We're leaving out the fact that a lot of these things have negative cost, because the payback time isn't long once our buildings are better insulated.

In Canada, 30 percent of our greenhouse gases come from inefficient buildings, inefficient heating, lighting, and cooling. We have all the technology we need to fix that. We lack the political will. We waste, in this country, more energy than we use, so surely the first thing we should be investing in is improving energy productivity.

The problem with debating someone like Bjørn is that he sometimes relies on economists, but then distorts their work. He relies on Professor Richard Tol to say that the benefit of reducing a ton of carbon is only two dollars. But Professor Richard Tol says that is quite wrong. The two-dollar figure comes about only when you ignore all the uncertainties. Tol thinks the better figure is 28 dollars a ton, in terms of benefit.

So you have to look at the technology, the improvements, the societal breakthroughs that we can make. But it starts with a commitment to decarbonizing our economy. As Sheik [Ahmed] Yamani once said, the Stone Age didn't end because we ran out of stones. It ended because we found something better.

BJØRN LOMBORG: So you agree. Come on over to this side.

RUDYARD GRIFFITHS: George, mankind lives in a variety of

temperatures around the globe. Could warmer temperatures lead to higher crop yields, to fewer winter deaths? Explain to us why you are so convinced that fast-rising CO_2 levels could mean a much more apocalyptic future.

GEORGE MONBIOT: Well, in the IPCC report, which Nigel Lawson obviously relies on in some respects, it says that beyond three degrees of warming, we have a net decrease in global food production. And those very simple and almost innocent-sounding words hide a really, really big story.

We know that the global population is likely to rise to 9 or 10 billion people during this century. We know that already it is quite difficult maintaining enough food for everybody in the world. Eight hundred million people go hungry all the time, even when we have a global food surplus. Try to picture what it would be like if there were a global food deficit.

That simple formulation suggests that the world can potentially go into structural famine. If that is the case it makes all the other things we're talking about — all of these are very big issues in their own right — look like sideshows at the circus of human suffering.

Of course we need to deal with hunger and poverty and disease. But let's not create these false choices. Let's not say it is one or the other. We have to do both. The reason that climate change is the overriding crisis is that unless we deal with it we simply cannot deal with these other issues and they will build up.

To address Rudyard's question, a little bit of warming might be a very fine thing in Canada, and there are an awful lot of people who could support it. But you can't have the warming in Canada without other countries experiencing warming. And in other places around the world, particularly in the Sahelian region of Africa, which is extremely vulnerable to drought, two degrees of warming would be catastrophic. This is why the first instance is a moral choice.

BJØRN LOMBORG: We need to do something for people in the Sahelian region of Africa and other places. How much will cutting carbon emissions help them? It's going to get warmer and warmer. There are going to be more and more problems for them. But George is going to save them by about 0.1 degrees towards the end of the century. It's a very inefficient way to help them.

He's essentially saying we should leave them as they are, instead of saying, "What if we actually tried to make sure that they could live better lives where they didn't have to deal with disease, where they didn't have to deal with lack of infrastructure, lack of education, lack of food?" They would live better lives, and, yes, they would also have to deal with global warming. But they would be able to do so in a manner that was closer to how industrialized countries do.

GEORGE MONBIOT: When did I say that we should leave those people as they are?

BJØRN LOMBORG: I'm pointing out that there is a much more effective way of helping people in the developing world. If you remember, George, in his introduction, said, maybe developed countries will deal with climate change, but poor countries won't. That's probably true. But the real issue is, should we then focus on doing something about climate change and leave these people poor? Or should we try to make them richer?

It turns out that every time that George, through his climate change policies, can save one person from starvation, the same amount of money spent on agricultural policies and making sure that people were better fed would save 5,000 lives. Yes, lives matter, and I would like us to save 5,000 lives rather than just one.

LORD NIGEL LAWSON: I'll try and make two quick points. The great killer — if you're interested in human life, and we all are — is poverty. Poverty is the problem. Acute poverty leads to malnutrition and exposure to diseases. All experience shows that economic aid can do a little bit, but the thing that gets people out of poverty is economic development. That's how we got out of poverty in the Western world, and that is how China, gradually, is doing it now.

To slow down that escape from poverty and all the ills that come with it by forcing the developing world to have more expensive energy is an immoral course. May I also point out that George totally misled you about the IPCC report on food production. It did not say that after a three-degree rise in temperature, you would have a net loss in food production — it didn't say that at all. What it says is that as the planet gets warmer — if it does, and it might well — up to a three-degree rise, then food production would be improved. After that, they think that food production would still be higher than it is today, but it would not be as helpful as if it were to somehow stop at three degrees. That's quite a different fact, and it's very important to get these things right.

Another thing the IPCC report considers is health. It's very interesting. They don't give any publicity to this, but the IPCC has a report which gives health outcomes on three different levels — virtually certain, very likely, and likely. The only health outcome that the IPCC believes to be virtually certain due to warming is reduced mortality from cold exposure. That is the only health outcome that they regard as virtually certain. You don't hear that often.

So there are great benefits from warming, as well as disadvantages. And that is why the net effect is likely — the IPCC's own figures show this — to be very small. The cost of trying to arrest [warming] by cutting back drastically on carbon dioxide emissions would be massive. Nobody in their right mind would want to go that way.

RUDYARD GRIFFITHS: I want to ask George to rebut Nigel's statement, but let me first ask the question. China took hundreds of millions of people out of poverty by burning dirty coal. What is the argument for not doing that, for the potential cost of being able to raise people out of poverty?

GEORGE MONBIOT: I want to see all of the world's poor people have much more access to energy than they have today. But I don't want there to have to be a trade-off between them having access to energy and them having access to the food and water that are required for their survival.

We have great opportunities here. The Iraq War cost the

U.S. economy 3.2 trillion dollars. That could have electrified Africa with alternative technologies. And in many parts of Africa it's a lot cheaper to build solar panels and batteries than it is to build a whole grid attached to fossil fuel power stations.

So there is this false choice being presented. Either you have poverty and you leave people to rot, or you have massive spending on fossil fuels and tremendous climate change. You can help people escape from poverty. You can give them all they need to have decent and prosperous lives without having to build hundreds of new coal-fired power stations, without having to continue mining fossil fuels which threaten those very lives that we are trying to protect.

Just so you know that I'm not making this up, I recommend that anyone who believes what Nigel says about the IPCC report read Table 19.1 in Chapter 19 of the report, which says that beyond 3 degrees global food supplies decrease. The way Nigel and Bjørn talk about it, it's as if everything is ultimately flexible, just as economists would predict. The price rises and therefore you can produce more of a particular commodity, you produce more and the price falls, so you produce less. The whole world just responds to those market signals.

But what if the water has run out? What if it has stopped raining in a region? What if, as I've seen in the northwest of Kenya, it hasn't rained for four years? How do you grow food? What technology can sort that problem out for you? You can't magic this stuff out of the air, you can't make it happen.

If climate change extends beyond a certain point, and the

point identified by most climate scientists is around two degrees of warming, it gets harder and harder for those fundamental needs to be met, whatever technology you throw at it.

A very large study, which took place in Britain, brought together by the Hadley Centre, suggested that with two degrees of warming, 2.1 billion extra people are subjected to water stress. That poses a tremendous problem, and we can't just magic that problem away on a spreadsheet. That's not how it works. This is the real world we're talking about.

Just like Bjørn, I'm absolutely in favour of investing a lot in new technologies and of developing renewable energies. But the problem is that dealing with climate change is not just a question of what you do, it's also a question of what you don't do. At the same time, we have to disinvest from fossil fuels. Otherwise it's like saying, "Well, okay, I've eaten two Big Macs and an ice cream and a chocolate fudge cake today, but I also had a salad. So why aren't I losing weight?"

We have to replace the chocolate fudge cakes and the Big Macs and the ice creams with the salad. And that means a concerted global program of action of the kind that we see at the Climate Conference in Copenhagen. Otherwise, all that happens is that the renewable energies supplement the fossil fuels rather than substituting them. That's not going to be good for anyone.

If we want to bring people out of poverty, let's do it, but let's do it with renewable energy. It's going to cost a lot, but so will a sustained commitment to fossil fuels, as history has shown. Thirty trillion dollars transferred to OPEC — why not spend that money instead on new technologies? If we're going to shell out trillions of dollars, let's make sure we spend it on the right things.

RUDYARD GRIFFITHS: I'm going to give Elizabeth the last word in this segment, and then we need to go into closing arguments and proceed to the second vote.

ELIZABETH MAY: The problem with this debate is that we're discussing an issue without really having discussed the context of why action is urgent on the climate crisis.

The key issue here is that the climate crisis is putting in motion some rather fundamental changes. And the kind of impact on humanity and ecosystems depends on stabilizing carbon dioxide in the atmosphere at a level to which we can adapt. Or do we wait and lose our chances? I'm completely in favour of a major effort at adaptation.

A big part of that effort can involve poverty alleviation. Quite frankly, the electrification of areas that currently don't have access to lights or clean water or many of the things that can be provided through decentralized energy supplies could be part of the strategy that responds to the climate crisis. Certainly, protecting the world's forests is moving faster now, under the agenda for the Climate Conference in Copenhagen, than it ever has before. Countries in the developing world whose largest contribution to greenhouse gases is loss of forests are now voluntarily asking for help in restricting deforestation.

So, yes, we need adaptation. We need poverty alleviation. We signed onto the Millennium Development Goals

211

[MDGs]. We've made no more progress there than we have on climate, and it really is a false choice to say that because we want to fight climate change we can't bother with the Millennium goals. Neither has achieved the kind of political salience that they need.

The window in which action makes any sense is a closing window. Our opportunity to avoid the worst case scenario of the climate crisis, so that we can focus on adapting to those scenarios we can no longer stop, is critical and urgent.

And frankly, when we talk about poverty and Africa, I think any Canadian would know that there is no Canadian who has been a greater humanitarian and worked more for Africa than Stephen Lewis.

And he does not agree with Bjørn, who — with all due respect, I don't know what you've ever done, but maybe you've done a lot for Africa. But Stephen Lewis says clearly, on top of all the poverty, on top of the pandemics, Africans are likely to experience more droughts, reduction of agricultural productivity, and famine, all because of climate change. Climate change is a nightmare for Africa.

RUDYARD GRIFFITHS: It's been a great exchange, and I want to allow each of our speakers to give their final arguments.

GEORGE MONBIOT: The reason I'm concerned about climate change is because of my experiences in northwest Kenya. I mentioned the region before, but I haven't told you exactly what happened.

When I was there in 1992, they were suffering the most severe drought they had suffered to date. Since then they've suffered two more droughts which have been even worse. And because of that drought, everyone was under the most extraordinary pressure. They had run out of basic resources, and the only option they had was to raid neighbouring tribes and take resources from them.

At one point, I was about to go up to the cattle camp that my Turkana friends and their families were running. And it had been stricken by a tremendous drought, and I fell very ill just before I was due to go up. I got malaria, and I collapsed on the street and eventually had to be taken away to Nairobi. And I thought it was a terrible misfortune that had befallen me. It was actually the luckiest thing that ever happened in my life. Because when I finally recovered, I went back to this cattle camp I was supposed to have visited before. I was with one of the relatives of the people in the cattle camp.

About ten miles before we got there, this man suddenly burst into tears, and he was screaming and wailing and crying, and I asked him what on earth was going on. And he said, "Can't you see?" And I said, "I'm sorry, I can't see." And as I got closer and closer, I did see. There were vultures hanging in the air just above this cattle camp. And when we arrived, all that remained of the ninety-eight people who lived there were their skulls and backbones. They had been eaten by hyenas. The Toposa people had come in the night and surrounded this cattle camp and machine-gunned it with AK-47s and G3 rifles. They killed ninety-six people that night. There were two that got away, and they killed them the next day. They killed them because they were desperate, and they were desperate because of the droughts. And that drought almost certainly was a result of climate change.

This is what we are up against. Not the esoteric abstractions and the figures and the squabbles we've been having over spreadsheets and computer programs and what this and that figure says. This is about life and death to these people — people I came to love and respect when I was there. And I was seeing that, which turned me into a climate change campaigner.

I was always switched on to social justice and environmental issues. But all these other things that I'd been fighting for all my adult life — getting people properly fed and preventing conflict and preventing disease — all that spending and that effort becomes wasted in the face of climate change. And when I was working there I was working with Oxfam in East Africa, and it was Oxfam who told me that climate change was the major problem. They said, "If we don't deal with climate change, forget the rest of our programs. We might as well pack up and go home."

And this is why Oxfam, along with Christian Aid and scores of other development agencies, are lobbying and bellyaching at the Climate Conference in Copenhagen and elsewhere. They are desperate to get their governments to respond to this massive crisis. These people who are most concerned with poverty and famine are telling us that climate change is mankind's defining crisis, and it requires a commensurate response.

BJØRN LOMBORG: Nobody doubts that George and Elizabeth and everybody else here have their hearts in the right place. That's not the question. The question is whether George, in his experience with the people who are suffering in northwest Kenya, is saying they are suffering because of global warming — I would be worried about making that connection right away, but let's just say that it is so and we should do something about global warming. What exactly is he saying?

Global warming will mean more drought, so the people in northwest Kenya will become more and more desperate. So why do we want to help them by making them slightly less desperate towards the end of the century? If we really have our hearts in the right place, wouldn't we want to make sure that they become more developed? And stop using the AK-47, and start having civilization that works for them and actually makes them able to feed and educate their kids? That is the fundamental issue.

That is why focusing on these issues is terribly important. It's not about saying, "This is the defining crisis for mankind." If anything, it's about making sure that we do the right things instead of just the things that feel right.

George Monbiot also told us that 2.1 billion people are going to be in water stress because of global warming. That's true. He failed to tell you that studies by Professor Neville Nicholls show that if there was no global warming, there would be 3.6 billion people in water stress. Actually, global warming in that particular area means that there will be less water stress, not more. Why? Because there will be more water vapour in the atmosphere.

So, there are a lot of studies and a lot of numbers flying back and forth, but we are simply not being well-informed if we are being told that this is the only and defining crisis.

Still, in some ways, I'm very encouraged by this debate.

Both Elizabeth May and George Monbiot actually moved over to our side during the course of the debate. George said he wants us to focus just as much on all these other areas, and yet climate change should be the most important issue. Of course, George is right. We should be focusing on all these things, and that, of course, means that you have to say this is not the defining crisis. It is one of the many crises on which we need to focus.

And Elizabeth said we need to make much greater investment into research and development of green energy technologies, because that is what is going to solve the world's problems. It is not about running out of stone. It is about finding smarter, new technology. I commend her for turning around and saying what does work. So we are, in some ways, already agreeing.

Let me sum up. Both of them mentioned Oxfam, and I think it is crucial that Oxfam told us that the leaders involved in the G8 Summit decided that they were going to spend about 50 billion dollars extra on climate change. They were going to take that money, it appeared at the time, mainly from overseas development aid. Oxfam representatives said, "This is terrible. If you take those 50 billion dollars, you're essentially going to make it impossible for us to save four and a half million children from dying. Yet if you spend it on climate change, you can postpone global warming by the end of the century by six hours."

I ask you, what is more important — to save the lives of four and half million children, or postponing global warming by six hours? That is the challenge. And so to put it very bluntly, Al Gore talks about global warming as being our defining moment. How do you want to be remembered by your children and grandchildren? By spending trillions of dollars to do virtually no good a hundred years from now, or by spending less money now and making a much better world? I ask you to reject the motion.

ELIZABETH MAY: Certainly during this debate we've heard some compelling arguments and some interesting theatre. But this issue is far more important and requires a serious analysis of the real science.

Bjørn plays with numbers and plays with facts in a way that I find deplorable. I've read both of his books and I've checked every footnote. Of course, I couldn't find any evidence to support the claims he made.

The truth of the matter is that credible scientists have a body of work that has persuaded the politicians of this world. And when you start with former Prime Minister of Canada Brian Mulroney and former Prime Minister of the U.K. Margaret Thatcher as early adherents, taking leadership that we must address the climate crisis, I invite you to imagine what would possibly have compelled them if it wasn't that the science was clear that we have to act. We've lost precious decades.

In this debate, for instance, you just heard Bjørn say that we would have fewer people with water stress. Well, there's no one in this world who has done studies that say that. The climate scientists around the world have made it very clear that the climate crisis will exacerbate access to water, and in those places where you have deluge events, so you'd say there's more water there, you can't capture it. You'd have to empty every reservoir to capture the excess water that suddenly appears, and it is like pouring water through sand.

It's like Mozambique. Mozambique had no rain for eight months, and it got its entire annual rainfall in one two-week period in 1998. It was a dreadful flood and lots of lives were lost. They couldn't capture the water that came in the two-week period. The nature of the climate crisis is that it will bring extreme water stress and it will create millions of environmental refugees. And, as many people around the world now recognize — including studies out of the Pentagon — we're looking at issues where the crisis itself is a profound threat to our security.

We haven't talked about some key science. I mentioned earlier ocean acidification, which is not temperature-related. It is the carbon dioxide in the atmosphere creating carbonic acid in the world's oceans, threatening life in our oceans. How do we feed the world's people or deal with the fact that we could be losing life in our oceans if we don't act?

Both Nigel Lawson and Bjørn Lomborg write in their books that there is no sign of the Antarctic ice melting. Yet some of the best science on the subject is being done right here at the University of Toronto. For example, the Gravity Recovery and Climate Experiment, GRACE. There was a presentation to parliamentarians that I recently attended in Ottawa, by Dr. William [Richard] Peltier, who is a scientist with the IPCC. And the information on the western Antarctic ice sheet is very clear. It is destabilizing, it is losing its mass. Sudden, abrupt climate change can't be modelled, but if the western Antarctic ice sheet were to go, sea level rise would rise nine metres in Canada. Figure out the economic cost to this country of a nine-metre sea level increase. It would be significantly more than the amount we could spend to ensure that we go off fossil fuels as quickly as possible.

We know about science. We know about debates. We know that there are limits on free speech. When you're in a crowded theatre, you don't shout "Fire." But when you're in a crowded theatre and you feel the floorboards warming under your feet and you see smoke clouding the exit signs and someone comes to the front and says, "Ladies and gentlemen, stay in your seats. That smoke you see is a malfunction in the popcorn machine. We really have no problem here. Bar the door and stay in your seats" — well, that's when people need to say, "I can still see the exit sign through the smoke." Now is when we act. Now is when we save lives.

LORD NIGEL LAWSON: I will be very brief. Let me make two fundamental points. And the water stress point is actually an interesting example of a whole lot of things right across the board.

As I said, there has been no warming so far this century — and that is a fact, though our opponents in this debate don't like it. They hate it. It's astonishing! They ought to be pleased. They ought to be delighted, but instead they're upset that there hasn't been this great global warming. If there were global warming, it might exacerbate water stress, but water stress has always been there. Drought has always been a problem. There has always been water stress. What are you going to do?

Global warming causes only a marginal exacerbation of

water stress and drought. Do you obsess over this marginal exacerbation or do you say, "We've got to attack the real problem. We've got to have better water resource management, have better storage facilities to capture water, not lose it. We've got to have, where it's effective, water pricing, in order to avoid the enormous waste of water that occurs throughout the world at the present time"? You attack the problem. You don't attack this minor exacerbation as the result of climate change.

However, I will make one concession; that they have the best of the rhetoric. I've been in politics for a very long time, and I have observed from time to time that there is somehow a gap between politicians' rhetoric and the reality. I hate to say that, but one or two of you may sometimes have discerned this difference. And I have to say, too, that I have never, during a very long life in politics — or before politics in journalism, writing about politics — known such a large gap between the rhetoric and the reality on an issue, where the politicians talk big but do very little.

And why is it? Because the rhetoric sounds wonderful, but, in fact, the cost of going the route they're recommending is prohibitive. The Chinese and the Indians can't afford it, and the electorates in the richer countries — well, I doubt whether they'll go along with it. We can see clearly that it is useless if it's not a global thing. The rhetoric is marvellous, as are the scary stories — every newspaper knows the scare stories sell newspapers, whether they are medical scare stories or anything else, so there is a tendency to talk in these terms.

But that's not the kind of politics I believe in. I believe in reason. I believe that it may be bad rhetoric, but I believe the only way we will actually help humanity is by using the power of reason and working out what is sensible and rational. And that is why I invite you to reject this motion.

SUMMARY: Lawson and Lomborg's arguments against the resolution were persuasive. Pre-debate votes were 61 per-cent in favour and 39 percent against the resolution, while the post-debate votes stood at 53 percent in favour and 47 percent against.

HEALTH CARE

Be it resolved that I would rather get sick
in the United States than in Canada.

Pro: Dr. William Frist and Dr. David Gratzer
Con: Dr. Robert Bell and Dr. Howard Dean

June 7, 2010

HEALTH CARE

INTRODUCTION: In light of the health bill passed in the U.S. in March 2010, many comparisons were made between the health care systems in Canada and the U.S. This debate continued that dialogue with many detractors and supporters in both countries.

It was a congenial conversation when four doctors took to the stage to debate the timely issue of health care. Two Canadians — Doctors Robert Bell, the President and CEO of the University Health Network, and David Gratzer, author and Senior Fellow at the Manhattan Institute — and two Americans — doctors-who-double-as-politicians William Frist, Professor of Business and Medicine at Vanderbilt University and former U.S. Senate Majority Leader, and Howard Dean, six-term Governor of Vermont, former Democratic National Committee Chairman, and presidential candidate — wrangled over the following statement: Be it resolved that I would rather get sick in the United States than in Canada.

On the pro side were Frist and Gratzer, on the con side Dean and Bell. It was Frist who perhaps most surprised the crowd with his praise for President Barack Obama's political skills in having managed to pass his landmark health care reform bill, despite passionate opposition from some Democrats and Republicans. Frist pointed out that the bill would guarantee coverage for millions more Americans than were previously insured. That said, Frist and Gratzer both highlighted studies indicating that Americans have more access to the latest medical technologies and treatments, while Canadian hospitals and clinics lag behind. Bell and Dean both argued that social inequities in the private system rendered it, in the long term, not worth whatever benefits it offered. Bell moved the crowd by talking about his experiences working at a hospital in the United States, where he saw children from minority groups treated for cancer almost always at later stages than white children.

Ultimately, though, there was some agreement among all four parties. No one believed that an entirely private or socialized system of health care was desirable or even possible. Even in socialist paradise Sweden, Gratzer said, user fees were charged to those who used hospital emergency wards needlessly.

RUDYARD GRIFFITHS: I'm going to call on Senator William Frist for his opening statement.

WILLIAM FRIST: It's an honour to be here, and I think the real goal is to see the contrast, for you to learn, for us to have fun, so thank you for that opportunity. I'm speaking to the 83 percent of you who are willing to change your minds, not the other 17 percent. It has been a fascinating year in the United States. President Barack Obama pulled off what most Americans thought would be impossible. That was to propose, to help legislate, and ultimately pass a health care bill against great odds and in a very partisan way, which is unusual for big social legislation in America.

He also managed to pass a bill that extends coverage towards the Canadian ideal, universal coverage. Historically this has been a very real defect in our system. In the past sixty years, presidents and others had tried to change it. The one thing it did not do was lower the cost of health care. We'll come back to that, because both Canada and the United States must address it, or at least lower the cost curve, the growth of health care over time. That bill does nothing, or does very little in that regard.

Throughout the year-long debate, however, Canada's health care system was placed out there as an option, as a model of the single-payer, centralized control position. What is important, and hopefully you'll understand why, is that the model of a single-payer system was rejected by the President of the United States, by the Democratic and the Republican leaders in the United States Congress. It was rejected by the Democratic and the Republican leaders in the United States Senate and by the American people.

Why? It was rejected because if you get sick you want to be in America. We'll come back to expectations, but part of what's in the American psyche is not to have politicians — and you've got a couple of former politicians in this debate — or bureaucrats limiting in some way what kind of health care you can have for your daughter who is dying of leukemia.

That concept of having somebody else controlling a single spigot of resources that dictates convenience, or whether you can get to the best specialist, is simply something with which the American psyche is not comfortable.

Reviewing Canadian press coverage, you get a pretty dismal picture of America, and again, I'm not going to change that, especially with the 17 percent who voted "no" to the resolution. I think you are probably going to stick with what you believe. But I do want you to understand a little bit about how a pluralistic system works, and that it is rich and robust, and that it has benefits and advantages.

Our system is part socialized — our veterans' system — and is single-payer for a large number of people through Medicare. I'll come back and explain our Medicare and Medicaid.

In the U.S., we are the undisputed leader in biomedical research. We have a robust arsenal of prescription drugs as part of our Medicare plan. We have the best diagnostic and treatment technology in the world. And the good thing about it for the overwhelming majority of people is that it can be delivered more conveniently and with more certainty in the United States when you need it.

A quick primer on American health care: we've got a system that has about 42 million people on Medicare, which is a single-payer system run out of Washington, D.C., with a lot of price controls. We have a Medicaid system that has 47 million people. It is for low-income people, and not as complete as it should be. The new legislation adds another

16 million people to that over the next nine years. We have socialized health care in our system of veterans' administration. And then we have 170 million people out there who get private health care insurance through private plans.

Let me say something about the uninsured in the U.S. Today there are 46 million uninsured. Of those, 30 million are completely uninsured. Now, it's important to note that about 15 million of that 46 million earn more than 55,000 to 60,000 dollars a year and simply choose not to have health care insurance. If they need it they'll go out and buy it.

My experience as a heart and lung transplant surgeon really introduced to me the single most important thing that would be lost if we went to a single-payer system, and that is our capacity to innovate. Our capacity to innovate is funded in large part because of an environment in which we do spend more on our health care, and in which there is a for-profit motive. It is a virtue, not a vice.

In America we put a high value on innovation; it is part of the American spirit. And that happens through a vibrant private sector. What's the evidence? The U.S. produced eighteen of the last twenty-five Nobel laureates; thirty-two U.S. companies have developed half of all major new medicines introduced worldwide. And Americans played a key role in 80 percent of the most important medical advances over the last thirty years.

In America today you have access to the highest technology and the greatest biomedical research in the world.

RUDYARD GRIFFITHS: I'm now going to call on Robert Bell for his opening comments.

ROBERT BELL: Arguing against getting sick south of the border begins not with medical statistics, but rather by comparing bankruptcies in our two countries. Americans are nearly three times as likely to become bankrupt as Canadians, and the reason is medical bankruptcy.

David Himmelstein wrote in the *American Journal of Medicine* in 2009 that 62 percent of American bankruptcies were caused by an inability to pay medical bills. Surprisingly, he found that three-quarters of medical debtors had health insurance that proved inadequate to pay the bills in the face of a serious illness.

Nearly all medical statistics show better health outcomes in Canada. Johns Hopkins is an esteemed medical university in Baltimore, and their statisticians have compared national health results in Canada and the U.S. using Organisation for Economic Co-operation and Development [OECD] data. Life expectancy and infant mortality are better in Canada, health care costs 60 percent more in the United States, and, according to Johns Hopkins, Canadian patients live longer with cancer, heart disease, stroke, diabetes, and lung disease.

Furthermore, the Hopkins team found that the chance of dying from a medical error in an American hospital is 50 percent greater than in a Canadian hospital. So, if you get sick and you choose to go to the United States, you die sooner, you have a higher risk of fatal medical error, you pay at least 50 percent more, and if you are sick enough you go bankrupt.

However, rather than relying on statistics, let me tell you why as a surgeon I would rather look after sick patients in Canada than in the United States. I learned my specialty as a bone cancer surgeon at Massachusetts General Hospital, an affiliate of Harvard Medical School, and what I saw there made me come home to Canada to stay. Looking after teen-agers with bone cancer in Boston was troubling. Black and Hispanic children frequently came to our clinic at a much later stage of disease, with large tumours that frequently required amputation rather than arm- or leg-salvaging sur-gery, or even after cancer had spread to their lungs.

This demonstrated the poor health equity outcomes evi-dent even in Massachusetts, the most liberal state in the nation. This was also my first exposure to the inequity of American health insurance and health economics. Private insurance is the root of all evil, if you get sick, in America.

I used to be in charge of Princess Margaret Hospital, Canada's leading cancer research centre, and I frequently visited The University of Texas MD Anderson Cancer Cen-ter, our counterpart in Houston, to exchange research ideas. Both hospitals treat about the same number of new patients. But there were two areas where there was a huge difference between the two hospitals: in the billing office and in chemo-therapy treatment.

The billing office at Anderson had 500 employees furiously negotiating payment terms with multiple insurance compa-nies. At that time, Princess Margaret employed one person in our billing office to collect for private rooms and televisions. Everything else was covered by our universal health insur-ance, showing why health care administration costs 3 percent in Canada compared to 13 percent in the United States.

Anderson also had more patients in chemotherapy treat-ment than at Princess Margaret, at least in part because of medical economics. U.S. cancer centres make a large profit from administering chemotherapy since they charge a substantial markup on chemotherapy drugs. This may explain why you are much more likely to get multiple courses of chemotherapy in America than in Canada, even though more lives are lost to cancer in the U.S., according to Johns Hopkins. The extra chemotherapy may not extend your life, but it sure makes big profits for the cancer hospital.

In closing, the U.S. has excellent health professionals; many of our doctors have studied — as I did — in the U.S. However, many American doctors come to Toronto, to Canada, to study with Canadian experts such as heart surgeon Dr. Tirone David at the Peter Munk Cardiac Centre. Dr. Frist himself is a cardiothoracic surgeon who practised lung transplant surgery prior to entering politics, and has told us during this debate about the importance of innovation and developing new therapies in transplants.

The senator knows, however, that the first successful single and double lung transplant operations in the world were done at Toronto General Hospital, and we continue to have the best results in the world in our University Health Network Multi-Organ Transplant Program.

Health care in both countries stimulates steamy debate. As Bill Maher recently said, "If conservatives get to call universal health care 'socialized medicine,' then I get to call private for-profit health insurers 'soulless vampires making money off human pain.'" Those vampire insurers have launched a false information campaign against Canadian health care, suggesting that our patients wait for days in emergency departments and years for elective surgery.

In my final remarks I'm going to tell you the truth about

Ontario wait times. And later tonight I'm going to introduce you to the man in this audience who has contributed more than any Canadian since Tommy Douglas to a sustainable health system in this country. But for now I want you to know that I am happy to work as a surgeon in a system that provides care based on patient need rather than insurance company and health care provider profit.

RUDYARD GRIFFITHS: David, you are up next.

DAVID GRATZER: By night, I'm a father and an insomniac. When my daughters are put to bed I like to write about health care policy. By day, I'm a physician and a Torontonian and I see patients in the Greater Toronto Area. Like so many physicians who work in Toronto I do the best I can to put my patients first. But too often I fear we have a system that puts politics first.

In countless decisions about technology, human resources, access to care itself, politics takes priority over the health care needs of our patients. Wait times are the best example of this. Over the last decade, three federal governments have demanded service guarantees and better wait times in exchange for new funding. The federal government's own wait list watchdog insists that seven out of ten provinces — seven — have yet to deliver on those promises.

But the funding came through. In the last ten years Ontario's health care spending has doubled, Nova Scotia's has doubled, Alberta's has tripled over eleven years, and yet what did we get for our money? In many cities patients still wait for the care they need.

To help you understand what waiting for surgery may feel like, let's do a bit of a demonstration. I like to make things interactive. Is everyone ready?

First of all, introduce yourself to the person on your left. Now, here's a quick anatomy lesson — and I'm a psychiatrist, so this is going to be a very quick anatomy lesson. Your knee has a big bone above it called the femur, and a little bone right under it called the tibia. And the stuff that holds all this together and makes it work is the cartilage. Now, lean over towards your neighbour to whom you've just introduced yourself and tear out the cartilage from their left knee.

Now you've got a lack of cartilage in your left knee and you have an understanding of why a knee replacement is so important. What you know is that now nights are going to be filled with pain, it will be difficult to walk and run and work and drive a car.

So here's the good news. If you're in rows A through Q raise your hands. Go ahead, raise your hands. Good news for you guys. According to the provincial government's wait time data, we'll fix your knee — if you go to Mount Sinai Hospital — by July 22. If you go to Sunnybrook Hospital it won't be until November 16. If you go to Sir William Osler Health Centre it will be December 13.

Those of you in rows R through U will wait longer than we clinically recommend. If you're from Markham, Ontario, you could wait past mid-January. Now, remember, this is all just a demonstration. But for those of us waiting for a knee replacement I want to point out that the wait times here in Ontario exceed all expectations by national and provincial standards. And this is a success story in the Canadian system — waiting months, possibly to 2011.

I could have picked more dire circumstances: cancer surgery in Hamilton, bypass surgery in Edmonton, hernia repair in Halifax. But I wanted to pick this example for a couple of reasons. First, seven out of ten provinces — seven — can't even meet that standard which they had agreed to measure by their own data.

Secondly, I want to mention an academic paper. A team at Laval University looked at 197 patients waiting for knee replacement surgery in Ontario and Quebec in 2008 who were in so much pain and anxiety that they recommended pre-surgery rehabilitation and mental health services.

Here's my point: we wait not only for knee replacements, we wait for practically everything in the Canadian system. You've heard time and again that a little bit of pain and anxiety is a small price to pay for the world's best health care, and it's free at the point of use. It isn't necessarily free at the point of use anymore, and it's not necessarily the best. You already know that the Americans do three times as many magnetic resonance imaging [MRI] scans as we do per capita, and twice as many computerized tomography [CT] scans.

What about positron emission tomography [PET] scanners? Some of you may not have even heard of it, it's so obscure in Canada. In 2008 there was a study of colon cancer treatment[3] showing half of doctors treated patients in

---

[3] The study appeared in the *Journal of Nuclear Medicine*, Vol. 49, no. 9 (September 2008), and is called "PET Changes Management and Improves Prognostic Stratification in Patients with Recurrent Colorectal Cancer: Results of a Multicenter Prospective Study."

Australia and New Zealand significantly differently after PET scan data. PET scans are only now being funded by OHIP, and I must point out that there were over 1,000 PET scanners in the United States by 2007.

Canada is even falling behind in key preventive measures. A joint Canada–U.S. survey of health found Americans have better access to preventive tests and higher treatment rates for chronic illness. We lag behind the U.S. and Europe when it comes to approving and insuring advanced drugs to treat cancer or rare disorders.

The political compromises that have been made are hazardous to your health. One way of comparing health care systems is to look at cancer outcomes. Five-year cancer outcomes in Canada — these are national statistics from a federal database — are 58 percent for men, and for American men it is 66 percent. For women there's less of a spread — 62 percent versus 62.9 percent.

The American system is complicated and deeply flawed but it's rich in resources, it's rich in research capacity, professional capacity, and care capacity, and if you don't believe me, your government certainly does. Ontario spent 164 million dollars last year sending our patients to their hospitals, because in the best health care system in the world we didn't even have the capacity to care for our sick.

That's not counting all of the people who are covered by OHIP and went to the United States hoping eventually the Canadian government would cover their care. There is, in a sense, a secret, private for-profit hospital here, and it's called the United States.

RUDYARD GRIFFITHS: Mr. Dean, your opening statement, please.

HOWARD DEAN: We've heard a lot of things about these systems. Let's talk about what the Americans think about their
system. Sixty-five percent of the people in America like their
health insurance. Thirty-five percent of Americans either
don't have any health insurance or have lousy health insurance where, if you should happen to get sick, you could lose
your health insurance because they don't have any obligation
to keep it. So we may be able to understand why, at least for
35 percent of Americans, and you'll have to guess which ones,
Canada may be a much better place if you happen to get sick.

Now, there is a lot of talk about three times as many computerized axial tomography [CAT] scans done in the United
States on a per capita basis. There are also three times as many
coronary artery bypasses done on a per capita basis in the
United States. If we start measuring the quality of our health
care by how much gets done to you, I think we're in trouble.

It may well be that those extra 200 percent of CAT scans
and coronary artery bypass graphs are unnecessary medicine promoted by a pay-for-service system which is completely out of control in the U.S. It is safer to get sick in
Canada because you may not have a whole lot of stuff done
to you that is unnecessary medicine.

And why is there unnecessary medicine? It is because
there's the potential to make a lot of money when doctors
can charge the insurance companies for all these procedures
whether they work or not, or whether you need them or not.

And why are so many extra procedures carried out in the
United States? Because we have a malpractice system that

is very different than the Canadian system, and people like me are encouraged to do as many things as possible so we don't see you in court and have to explain why we didn't do all those tests. You are better off in Canada and your wallet is better off in Canada.

We know, from my esteemed colleague Dr. Bell, that your outcomes are better in Canada, embarrassingly even for child mortality, which is really a moral disgrace. You are less likely to have invasive procedures in Canada, which may not be necessary. In terms of waiting times, I'm about to have my hip replaced. I decided to do so eighteen months ago.

Many of the processes that require waiting time in Canada require waiting time because they don't need to be done right away. I have no objection to having wealthy Canadians who want what they want immediately — which is an American disease — coming to the U.S. to have procedures. But if Canadians want a system which is 70 percent cheaper than ours and covers everybody, I think you are better off in the system that you have right now.

Is the U.S. health care system perfect? No. Is the Canadian health care system perfect? No. They both use pay-per-service medicine. That's a substantial problem that drives costs up, and driving costs up is a huge issue in Canada and in the United States. But you are starting from a lower base in terms of what it costs and a much higher base in terms of how many people are covered, which in Canada is 100 percent. That makes this country better not only than the United States of America in terms of coverage but better than France, Britain, and better than many other countries which supposedly have universal health care.

Let's talk about bureaucrats deciding what kind of health care people get. You say that politicians decide what kind of health care people get. I practised medicine for ten years. Not one time did I have to call my senator for permission to do a particular procedure, but I did have to call an insurance company bureaucrat who decided. They don't have an RN, they don't have an MD, and they've never seen a patient. Why are they telling me that I can't do a procedure on a patient? They are telling me because they will make more money if I don't. There is a profit incentive in the insurance system in the United States to do things that doctors think need to be done. I'll leave it to you whether that happens in Canada, but you don't have any health insurance companies, so I know an insurance company bureaucrat is not making those decisions for you.

Finally, let me just say that I would disagree with Senator Frist. The U.S. did not reject a single-payer system. We already have about 50 million people on a single-payer system. Our single-payer is bigger than your single-payer system. The mistake was we didn't let people under sixty-five choose our single-payer system, which is Medicare.

People in the Tea Party were saying government is too big, and we hate the government — but keep the government's hands off my Medicare. I went to a Tea Party meeting and there were 2,700 people there. I asked them how many people were on Medicare and about 40 percent raised their hands. I asked them how many people would willingly give up Medicare. About five people raised their hands. I think three had early dementia.

Government care is not as bad as it looks. We have a

socialized system, as William Frist pointed out. It's the veterans' care. What he didn't point out is that it is the number one–rated health care system by the patients of any health care system in the United States of America. It is a socialized system. And who's in it? The people who defended the United States with their lives, the Armed Forces of the United States. Not a bad system, and maybe one that more of us ought to be able to choose.

The fundamental problem with the American health care plan and the reason you're better off getting sick — if you have to get sick — in Canada is that our system is incredibly complicated. Insurance companies who decide between your health and their profit are running the vast majority of it. Americans are forbidden from choosing systems that have worked very well elsewhere.

The fact of the matter is, we have two great countries, but this is going to turn out like the Olympic hockey game.

RUDYARD GRIFFITHS: Please rebut anything you've heard in your opponents' opening statements. Senator Frist, you're up first.

WILLIAM FRIST: A lot will be made of outcomes and where the outcomes are best. We're not going to be able to go through each one, for cancer, for cardiac disease, length of life, infant mortality. Just be aware, because our papers — the *New York Times* and others — report we spend twice as much in the United States per capita than any other country and our outcomes are not as good because people don't live as long and we have higher infant mortality, and therefore we need a single-payer system, we need universal health care.

Well, let's have a look at that, because how long you live is not determined by how good a surgeon William Frist is or how good Toronto General Hospital is or whether you have universal health care or whether you have private insurance.

The number one factor determining how long you live is behaviour. Unfortunately, in the United States we have more homicides, and more accidents; behaviour such as smoking and obesity is more common across the board. Number two is genetics. There's more heterogeneity there. If you factor in behaviour and if you factor in genetics, and you actually correct for those, people live longer in the United States of America than in Canada. So beware of the statistics.

ROBERT BELL: I want to come back to what Howard was talking about, that's the issue of judging systems by the amount of care provided. How many people in this room have ever had back pain? Virtually 85 percent of the room has had back pain. How many of you have had an MRI? How many of you did anything differently based on that MRI? I don't see any hands going up.

HOWARD DEAN: One, I see one lady. So 2 percent of the people that had MRIs will have suddenly discovered they require surgery. I remember this from my training. Most of you have degenerative back disease; you need a physiotherapist, perhaps even a chiropractor, somebody who can tell you how to look after your back. You don't need an

MRI. Thirty percent of the MRIs that are done in this province aren't needed.

DAVID GRATZER: Maybe I'll just focus on Dr. Bell's argument, which is really based on two studies. They're important studies. The first is, of course, the Johns Hopkins University report on health outcomes. I'm going to deconstruct that report.

The second is the study on medical bankruptcy in the United States. David U. Himmelstein is one of the authors of the study, and he is somebody who publishes prolifically. I think when there is a suggestion of medical bankruptcies in the United States being so dramatic, it's worth a look.

Himmelstein gets the big publications, but doesn't withstand the great scrutiny so well. And as you know, the *New England Journal of Medicine* published a paper deconstructing his study. Amongst other problems with it, medical bankruptcy was declared by Himmelstein as anyone carrying a medical debt of over a thousand dollars at the time of declaring bankruptcy.

It's an absurd standard, and, in fact, one discovers that if you look at straight comparison between Canada and the United States, there are actually more bankruptcies in Canada than there are in the United States. The Department of Commerce statistics are 0.2 percent in the United States in 2006, 0.27 percent in 2007 versus 0.3 percent and 0.3 percent in Canada. Medical bankruptcies exist in the United States, and too often they exist here too.

HOWARD DEAN: I'm going to tell a quick story. I'm not going to do a lot of rebutting here; I think Robert Bell did a nice job of that. I had the good fortune of interviewing a young lady who actually is here at one of the Toronto hospitals — she's an American, she trained in the United States, she's moved up here.

Here's what she said: "Medicine is a lot more fun to practise here. You spend a lot less time doing paperwork." She said she spends three hours a day less doing paperwork here than she did doing paperwork in the United States.

She also told me the following story. When she was practising in Boston she admitted a young child who had the possibility of a birth injury from the obstetrics people. She was upbraided by her supervisor — she's a pediatric neonatologist — because she hadn't asked for an ultrasound of the head. She said, "Why ask for that, it's not necessary." They said because if you get sued you don't want to spend your time in court. We'll make the obstetrics people spend their time in court.

The truth is that most of the doctors I've talked to — at least the primary care people — would rather practise in Canada than they would in the United States. And the question is, do you want to be in a country where people are happier practising? I would say yes, because if they are they're probably doing better for you.

RUDYARD GRIFFITHS: Let's get into some specific questions and let's start with David Gratzer. In Canada we're spending 11 percent per capita GDP, versus 17 percent in the U.S., and not only are we living longer in Canada but we're living for more years free of chronic disease. So isn't that a hands-down argument for the single-payer system?

DAVID GRATZER: You haven't persuaded me. First of all, Americans undoubtedly spend more on health care than we do. But one has to take these things with a grain of salt. When you make a direct GDP comparison, one doesn't take into account, for instance, the medical legal environment one would have in the United States, and the fact that so much of medicine is practised as defensive medicine.

One also needs to bear in mind how much research and development is done in the United States. I'll bet if you look at a cancer centre like MD Anderson, it has a larger research and development budget than Canadian centres combined. Again, that's not to suggest that Canada doesn't have points of extraordinary excellence here, but if you're talking about a pharmaceutical drug being researched for a breakthrough in cancer, odds are it is in the United States. If you're talking about research being done on schizophrenia, odds are it is in the United States. Most of the breakthroughs in medicine are taking place in the United States. They're doing the world's research and development, so some of that is unfair because it speaks to legal issues rather than the health care system. I'm not persuaded that simply because they spend more they're wasteful. A lot of that money goes to good causes.

What about life expectancy? Senator Frist brought up a very good point. Let's be totally frank about it: Canadians are a little bit dull compared to our American counterparts. We tend to shoot up less than Americans. We tend to shoot each other less than Americans. And I'll be very polite to my American colleagues on this panel. How do we say this? When we go to McDonald's we tend not to supersize the way Americans do. The obesity rate is about 30 percent in the United States. It's unacceptably high. In Canada it's only 20 percent.

Now look, there are some really smart people, much smarter than me. Dr. Robert Ohsfeldt and Dr. John Schneider, both social scientists, did the following: they looked at life expectancy across the Western world, and they noticed that Americans are more likely to die in car accidents. That has nothing to do with the health care system. When you do a comparison of life expectancies you discover that life expectancy is longer in the United States than in any other country.

Here's the point: life expectancy is a very crude statistic. That's why I don't use it. That's why I look at disease outcomes. That's why I think they are a better standard.

HOWARD DEAN: I think there is a lot of selective use of information here and so, even though I don't happen to agree with what David said about life expectancy, let's just assume that he may be right. That may be true of the end of life, but it certainly isn't true of the beginning of life.

The U.S. has a much higher infant mortality rate than you have in Canada. Maybe you'd rather get sick in the United States, but I would think you'd much rather that if your children got sick — God forbid — it would be in Canada.

WILLIAM FRIST: It's important to recognize what David said: these very gross global measures don't capture universal care versus non-universal care, or any type of health insurance, or even type of facility itself.

Once again, if you compare the cost of socio-economic

conditions such as people living in poverty, drug use, and abusive drug use, and if you correct for low birth weight from Canada to the United States, the United States sky-rockets with a much lower infant mortality rate than in Canada. Once you correct for the other variables which have nothing to do with universal versus non-universal, or single-payer or pluralistic system, the numbers are different. So be careful.

HOWARD DEAN: Essentially the argument you're making is that we should prefer our health care in the United States, but then we should live like Canadians. This is nonsense. The fact that this country is deeply committed to the idea that every person ought to have universal health care has something to do with the mortality rates at both ends of life.

ROBERT BELL: Let me just jump back to what David suggested, and that is that the high cost of health care in the U.S. is related to innovation. Well, it goes back a long way, but you will remember when insulin was first used on a patient. You'll remember that stem cells were discovered by Dr. James Till and Dr. Ernest McCulloch at the Ontario Cancer Institute, leading to hundreds of thousands of people around the world having life-saving bone marrow transplants for leukemia.

I mentioned the fact that the first single and double lung transplant operations were done at Toronto General Hospital. I'll also mention that advances for gene therapy in doubling the number of lungs available for transplant have been made by the same team in the last year and are now being used in Pittsburgh, Birmingham, and around the world.

David, America is a wonderful and innovative place full of wonderful scientists, but so is Canada.

RUDYARD GRIFFITHS: Let's move on to innovation. The question for you, David and William, is that when you look at the cost of health care in both Canada and the United States, technology is right up there. Is technology the Achilles heel of the American system?

WILLIAM FRIST: Let me start, because this is worth spending time on. We've just heard five good anecdotes. But in 2001 a survey was done of great medical advances. And it showed that in the last three decades two thirds of those medical advances came out of the United States of America. One third came out of Europe. I'm not sure if Canada had any advancements or not.

In pharmaceutical development, twenty-five breakthrough drugs — these are the drugs that are going to be used by Canadians, not paid for by you, paid for by the American taxpayers to your benefit — were discovered in the United States of America or by scientists who came to America because of our robust, innovative research system.

In part, the U.S. spends more for health care because we know the benefits. Canada does a pretty good job in adopting some of the technologies, even though it's amazing to me to hear that CT scans and MRI scans are not important. It was also amazing to hear my driver — coming in yesterday from the airport — telling me anecdotally how long he has to wait for a CT scan for a headache that's the worst he's ever had.

It's amazing to me that we're arguing that less technology, innovation, and health care are to your benefit. That's not the case in America.

ROBERT BELL: Senator, I would suggest that technology is not innovation. Innovation is technology applied to cost-effective health improvement. There can be new machines invented every day. A great example is PET scanning. PET scanning was not approved in Ontario until very recently because the studies done in Ontario demonstrated diseases where PET scanning made a difference.

WILLIAM FRIST: If they are so bad, why are you putting one in your hospital?

ROBERT BELL: We've got three, because we treat a lot of those diseases —

WILLIAM FRIST: And you want more!

ROBERT BELL: You're doggone right. But what I'm saying is that the adoption of best evidence practice to actually define where new pharmaceuticals and new technology — diagnostic or therapeutic — make a cost-effective difference to outcomes is the true thing that improves the health care system. Otherwise it's seduction by the companies developing new technology, seduction to physicians that simply want to provide new toys to play with in diagnosing their patients. And unless they can demonstrate that there is an improvement in their patients —

WILLIAM FRIST: Why do you have, or are putting twelve CT scans in your one facility? You're saying this is bad, so why are you doing it? Why did you show me — and it was impressive — what you've done there with the most technologically advanced system in the world, if technology is so bad? You don't get your money from government and you don't get it from the private sector. You get it from philanthropy.

In America the taxpayers pay for developments by paying more for their health care. It's important for people to understand that innovation, technology, and research and cures for Alzheimer's and cures for HIV someday are going to come from the United States of America. They aren't going to come from Canada or from Europe. They're going to come from America, in part because we pay more.

HOWARD DEAN: I think this is a great argument, but the fact of the matter is that it argues why the U.S. should be in the Canadian system. The U.S. is going to pay for all of this innovation, and that makes for a hell of a big discount for Canadians.

WILLIAM FRIST: I agree.

RUDYARD GRIFFITHS: David, are we in Canada a nation of free riders or are we being smart?

DAVID GRATZER: Look, being a free rider is great as long as you get the goods right up front. Being invited to your aunt's for Thanksgiving is good if you get to eat at the dinner table. It's no good if you have to wait for cold turkey for breakfast the next morning.

And I'm afraid, Dr. Bell, I'm going to have to agree to disagree with you here. Of course what we want is cost-effective medicine, but in Ontario and across Canada what we have is a system that is technologically phobic in part because we are private investment-phobic. We'll hesitate, we'll study, and our bureaucrats will stall. It's part of their way of rationing the supply of health care.

New is not necessarily better, but new can be critically better. Look at the medical revolutions of the last sixty years — and when we talk about modern medicine we're not talking about the last six thousand years or the last six hundred years. We're really talking about the last sixty years. What we've done — changing childhood leukemia from a death sentence to an eminently treatable condition, eliminating polio, turning depression into an eminently treatable condition — are, for the most part, things that have to do with new drugs and new technologies.

PET scanners are a great example. You and I both know that in treating specific cancers they are critical to our understanding, and that's why finally our government agreed to fund this new technology. But what happened to the people who needed that technology in 2004, in 2005, 2006, or in 2007? They were told, "Tough luck," and some of them went to the United States.

ROBERT BELL: David, let me ask you a question. What is the most innovative therapy being investigated today for chronic refractory depression? It is neuro-stimulation.

DAVID GRATZER: I knew you were going to say that because it comes from your hospital. I watch *60 Minutes* too, and you guys do great product placement. I'm not actually sure that I agree with you, though. I'm a psychiatrist, I'm not a surgeon. But you can't cut and stimulate —

ROBERT BELL: Innovative research, it happens in Canada.

RUDYARD GRIFFITHS: Let's shift to something that we discuss a lot in Canada, and that's wait times. Robert, let me start with you.

The Ontario Health Quality Council came out last week with a report saying that only 53 percent of urgent cancer surgeries are being performed within the recommended time, some 750,000 Ontarians do not have a GP, nine out of ten people in Ontario say they are waiting too long to see a doctor. In a single-payer system, are these kinds of statistics permanent structural features?

ROBERT BELL: Absolutely not. There's a change that's occurred across the Canadian health system that is probably the most significant in Ontario, where there is a concept of measuring outcomes, measuring access to care, looking at the root causes of the problem, and making targeted investments. What we call in Ontario "pay-for-results."

Four years ago wait times in Ontario emergency hospital

departments were terrible. I'm going to tell you later what they are today, thanks to the Ontario Wait Time Strategy. Alan Hudson, the lead within the Ontario Ministry of Health and Long-Term Care on Access to Services and Wait Times, is the most significant Canadian since Tommy Douglas in terms of creating a sustainable health system because he's shown us that you have to do root cause analyses, and you have to make targeted investments. You can't just throw money at the problem. For example: you have to improve the processes of care that allow the elderly not to stay in acute care hospitals for longer than they need to, but rather achieve some kind of community care for them which also frees up the system.

We are involved in a noble experiment — a Canadian publicly funded universal health system is a system that's defined by cost-effectiveness. We don't throw money at problems. We make targeted investments. That's a new approach. And I think it's the thing that is going to make this system sustainable for our children and our grandchildren.

RUDYARD GRIFFITHS: William, statistics show that you've got shorter wait times in the U.S., but again the equity in terms of access to the system is a major issue. If you were sitting here unaware of your place in the world, wouldn't you prefer the Canadian system?

WILLIAM FRIST: I disagree with the assumption or the premise that Canadians have better access to care. I spent twenty years in medicine doing things like heart transplants, which were very expensive at the time, and they were not covered here. Out of 150 heart transplants I've done, 40 percent were on individuals living under the poverty level.

I say that because the impression is always that the uninsured in the United States don't get care. And they do get care. Being insured matters, and that's why the government has addressed that in the new legislation, which extends coverage to 32 million more people.

There are 30 million hardcore uninsured. So the equity issue is a real issue. But for the overwhelming majority of 250 million people, access to care is good, and it's not from a single spigot, which is what occurs when somebody at the top gives the hospital a budget and that budget is the criteria they're using throughout the year.

In America it is not done that way. There are various spigots. There is the private insurance spigot. There is the Medicare spigot coming from government. There's the Medicaid spigot which comes from individual states — about 50 percent of it is state resources and 50 percent is federal resources. So the flow of resources gives, in a pluralistic system, flexibility of access and of quality.

The quality of the outcomes always ends up being sort of a wash. The access issue is important, and in the United States the uninsured — and, yes, having insurance matters — do get care. Where do they get care? Through 6,000 community health centres that are predominantly for the uninsured, and through emergency rooms. Once you hit that emergency room door — and, yes, you should be seeing primary care, and we have a primary care shortage in the U.S., just like Canada — you get equal care, regardless of where you might be on the socio-economic scale.

This was legislated in the 1990s. It may not be the ideal way to do it, it's inefficient, but the uninsured do get care in the United States.

RUDYARD GRIFFITHS: Howard, are you getting the best of both worlds? You are getting good access as well as quicker access.

HOWARD DEAN: Well, let me answer a question that you raised earlier. You said, is there something endemic about the single-payer system where you have to have wait times? The answer is no. We have a single-payer system for everybody over sixty-five in our country, and there are essentially no more wait times than there are for anybody else. I do believe not all the wait times, but a great many of the wait times, are probably something that is a good idea. The alternative is that you get whatever you want when you want it, and you look at those ads on television and you can go and give the doctor a list of all the medicines you expect to have prescribed to you within four minutes. And that is all the time you get to see the doctor in the United States, by the way. How long is your average office visit in Canada? It is six minutes in the United States. I'm not kidding, that's what happens when you have a private insurance market.

Let me briefly talk about unnecessary procedures. It is true that eventually most people who are uninsured get care. How would you like to get your primary care in an emergency room? Do you know the percentage of American medical graduates in 2008 that went into primary care? The answer: 9 percent. Does that tell you something about how unpleasant it is to practise if you're a primary care physician in the United States of America?

In Canada it's about 25 percent, which is still much too low. There is something about the American system which grinds out the people who are going to see you first in the medical system. Mostly I think it's the private insurance sector that grinds them down. So I do believe that the evidence is overwhelming that the Canadian system is better, and that the U.S. needs a system where at least we can give our folks a choice between the private system and the socialized system that's currently in place. Give us that choice and then our system will at least be what we want it to be.

RUDYARD GRIFFITHS: I want to move on to a final topic, a question for both teams of debaters. I'm going to start with our pro debaters first. I'm coming up on my fortieth birthday, and as part of Generation X our big question is, what kind of health care system is going to be around in twenty or thirty years?

WILLIAM FRIST: Let me comment on the American system and where we'll be. Our recent legislation added 32 million people to the insured. Sixteen million went into the government plan for Medicaid. Medicaid pays about 60 percent of the cost of taking care of a patient. It pays hospitals about 40 percent of the true hospital costs. So if you put everybody into that, the system would clearly implode. We would have no doctors or hospitals left in thirty years.

The other half went into the private sector through private sector exchanges and privatized plans, which gives a little bit of a feel for where the U.S. will be down the line. It will be a blended system. It will be multi-payer funded. It will give choice in terms of physician and in terms of plan — there'll be more transparency through a 20-billion-dollar investment and the part that we put in from the Obama administration for information technology.

Whether or not you are healthy twenty years from now, let me come back to a very important point. Your health is going to depend more on whether or not you smoke, whether or not you drive fast, whether or not you wear a seatbelt, whether you are obese, than it is going to depend on Toronto General Hospital or Massachusetts General Hospital or health care systems themselves.

ROBERT BELL: You're talking about that magic word "sustainability." Is the current system sustainable? There is a bit of an urban legend out there that it can't possibly be sustainable. How can it keep on growing? The answer is that there is no magic.

There are three things, three big cost drivers in the publicly funded health care system: hospitals, drugs, and doctors. Hospitals are pretty much getting under control — a 1.5 percent increase this year — but it's forcing us to find better ways to manage the 3 percent inflation that we're facing.

There may be pharmacists that are going to be upset if I say that the move on generic drug pricing is probably going to help us pull down costs, and my sense is that the Ontario Medical Association wants this system to be sustainable just as much as we do and they're ready to come to the table and talk. So don't believe that this is definitely an unsustainable system. I think there are all kinds of ideas being brought to bear right now which are going to provide us with better quality at better cost.

DAVID GRATZER: There is a really famous American economist by the name of Herbert Stein. Stein was a brilliant man. At one point in time he was actually an adviser to the President of the United States, and he coined Stein's Law of Economics. Stein's law says simply: that which cannot go on forever will eventually stop.

Okay, maybe it wasn't so profound, but when it comes to health policy it is profound. Canada has enjoyed really good economic times. Oil was trading at 150 dollars a barrel at one point in the last few years. And health spending has risen 8 percent annualized over the last decade. We won't have the type of investment in public health care the way we have had in the past. Difficult decisions will have to be made.

Our population is aging. A new Statistics Canada report suggests that there will be more seniors than children some time in the next half decade. As we move forward there are certain things Canadians need to do that our politicians don't like to talk about. One is to take health, not just health care, seriously, for the reasons that Senator Frist outlined. One in five Canadians is obese. They are opening themselves up to a slew of health costs that could be avoidable.

We need a role for the private sector in Canadian health care. The Labour government in Britain was able to contract out in a big way. In Ontario it's scandalous that there are no private MRIs serving public patients. And the third thing we need to do is have a meaningful discussion about patient cost-sharing. Every time these things get raised we hear that it is un-Canadian because it's an Americanization of our system. Fine, then what about a Swedification of our system? In Sweden, if you show up at the emergency department with a runny nose, you have to pay a user fee.

I also like experiments with medical savings accounts that you see in the United States. What I'm suggesting is that we should talk about those sorts of cost pressures instead of saying that what makes us Canadian is that we've got a free health care system that might leave you on a wait list.

The point of this system is not nationalism. The point of this system is to serve our patients. If Sweden has a good idea, let's look to Sweden. If Latvia has a good idea, let's look to Latvia. And if the United States has a good idea, that's okay, too.

RUDYARD GRIFFITHS: Howard, let's get you in on this question. Is there an advantage in the American system insofar as you have crossed the Rubicon a while ago in terms of individuals paying for their health care personally? And do you think a single-payer system like we have in Canada will exist twenty or thirty years hence?

HOWARD DEAN: There have been numerous people from a different party than I that have tried to undo Medicare, and their corpses are littered across the political scene, along with people who try to undo our social security. People love our health care system if they're in Medicare. The grass is always greener on the other side. Let us choose, if we're under sixty-five, to get into what people over sixty-five have. But what people over sixty-five have is essentially what every single one of you has.

There are faults. I agree with David that it wouldn't hurt to have co-pays. I mean there are economies of scale and some things that have to be done and incentives have to be changed. I think the pay-for-service system is a mistake for both countries. But the fact is you start with having everybody covered with health insurance. I don't think it's possible to know how valuable that is unless you live in a country for a while where everybody doesn't have health insurance.

RUDYARD GRIFFITHS: Let's go to some audience questions. First question to Robert. Why did Danny Williams, the Premier of Newfoundland, go to the U.S. for health care rather than seek service in the province that he governs?

ROBERT BELL: If I were the Premier of Newfoundland and I had to leave the province because the procedure wasn't available there, it might be easier to go to South Carolina than Toronto, where the procedure is also available. I'm not positive, but that may be the case. But I don't know exactly why he made that personal decision.

DAVID GRATZER: We all know that the premier left to have heart surgery in the United States, but we also know that many politicians do that. And it follows a relatively simple pattern.

First, they rail against the American system when they

run for office. Then they have a lump or a bump and go to the United States for care because they have looked at the same statistics I have, and then they come back and they feel really badly and some of them give Robert some money.

Let me be clear. I don't begrudge the premier for going to the United States. I dislike his hypocrisy. And I also wish that he would have had the opportunity in Canada to have a public versus private option. Instead of spending those health care dollars in Miami, I wish he had had the opportunity to spend them in St. John's.

ROBERT BELL: Canadians have a tendency to hide some of our light under a bushel. Former U.S. Senator Paul E. Tsongas talked about his life-saving bone marrow transplant and how he got that in Massachusetts and wouldn't have got it outside. In fact, bone marrow transplants were invented in Canada, and this is where stem cells were discovered. And yet we never really talk about that.

We don't brag about some treatments that Americans come here for — we have patients coming here to receive special surgeries they can't get in the United States, performed by doctors like Tirone David. There are a lot of Americans coming here for surgery.

DAVID GRATZER: It's also not so relevant to the overall debate. Let me say that Dr. David is an extraordinary individual. I did part of my training under Dr. Robert B. Zipursky, who might be the world's foremost expert in first episode psychosis. So what?

The point is that Canadians wait for care, and as a result, while we can find exceptions, we find a system so over-stretched that the Ontario government spends 164 million dollars a year taking our patients to the U.S. for treatment.

What you find when you're on a wait list here is that our political class opts out. It's the hypocrisy of living in Canada that you have to listen to Danny Williams drone on about why we have such a great system, but when it's his heart, he's on the next plane out of here.

I don't dislike Premier Williams. If he wanted to buy alcohol it would be legal. If he wanted to buy tobacco it would be legal. If he wanted to go to certain parts of Toronto at night and procure the services of a lady friend, for all intents and purposes it would be legal, and I think private health care is a lot better for your health — despite what Governor Dean has suggested — than it would be to buy tobacco, alcohol, or a lady friend.

WILLIAM FRIST: The United States of America is the number one tourist destination for advanced quality care in the world. That includes transplantation, that includes advanced cancer therapy, and that includes cardiac disease. It is the place that more people come to for advanced care.

ROBERT BELL: David, you mentioned the number of Ontarians who go to the United States for medical care. How many Americans go to Thailand and India practising medical tourism and get care that they can't afford and at reasonable quality in those countries?

HOWARD DEAN: Let me just say something about Premier Williams going to the U.S. for heart surgery in South Carolina. There are foolish consumers everywhere. Unfortunately, this debate plays into a Canadian national characteristic, which is that you assume that if somebody goes to the United States it means something bad about your system. In fact, he may have just done something really stupid.

I'm sure they have very nice care in South Carolina, but I'll tell you one interesting statistic. This is from the *New England Journal of Medicine* from fifteen years ago. For-profit health care delivers much worse results than not-for-profit health care. I don't think you have for-profit health care institutions in this country. Florida has the worst health care in America, and they have the highest percentage of for-profit institutions because they have got to make a lot of money so they do a lot of stuff.

So all I can say is Godspeed to the Premier of Newfoundland. I'm glad he came back in one piece.

RUDYARD GRIFFITHS: Aren't health care systems a reflection of a society's shared values, especially their concern for the least fortunate?

WILLIAM FRIST: The equity issue is important, and the United States is not perfect. But a pluralistic system is a system by definition that is fluid and that gives choice, and that will alter under a single-payer system. It's pluralism where you can innovate.

Things aren't going to work out if you put markets forward. And that is in part why a number of presidents, including President Obama, said, "Forget the cost of health care. We're not going to do anything about it. Even though health care is more expensive in the U.S. than in Canada and the population is growing three times faster than inflation, we are going to bring the uninsured to the table." For that I applaud him, but having some insurance does matter. So that's the law of the land in America and now, but the cost issue has to be addressed.

Dr. Dean wants to expand Medicare, which is a very popular system, a very generous system — more generous than your system in Canada — but it's not sustainable. Our single-payer system is going to go bankrupt. So that doesn't mean you sustain it, it means you improve it.

Part of that improvement that we haven't talked about that we need to talk about is changing health care into a more value-driven system. We need a system that is built around outcome and results per dollar coming in. And there are ways to do that. We didn't do it in our health care bill recently, but a value-driven system versus a volume-driven system is something on which I think we can all agree.

DAVID GRATZER: My job during this debate is not to whitewash the American system. My job here is not to suggest to you that it is a perfect system. Certainly I don't believe that. I wrote a book a couple of years ago talking about all the problems with the American system.

But I would suggest the following to you: we let ourselves off the hook too easily in Canada when we talk about problems in the American system. At least they've had a discussion about the uninsured. At least they've taken a step to address it. Here in Canada you'll never pay to see a family doctor. But getting to see a family doctor isn't so easy.

According to the Canadian Medical Association, four million Canadians — probably more — can't get a family doctor. There are towns here in Ontario where they hold lotteries and the people who win get to be taken in as patients by the town doctor. That's unacceptable, as I would suggest to you the uninsured problem in the United States is unacceptable and more needs to be done. We have significant access problems in Canada, too.

ROBERT BELL: What we've been engaged in is a discussion of the American and Canadian systems. We both need to be ashamed if we compare our systems to the Danish system, where every family doctor has an electronic record where patients can book their appointments online and get information from their family doctor by email as opposed to having to wait for a visit.

There's no question in the Canadian system that innovation is crucial to sustainability. My point of view, having talked to my colleagues who run American hospitals, is that our ability to innovate is far greater because we only have to deal with one insurance company. I don't know how many times I've heard an American CEO say something like, "We'd be able to send all those patients out to community care, except the insurance company won't provide us with co-pays and ..." I didn't even know what all the terms were when they were talking about insurance companies.

I think our ability here to talk to the people — the

democratically elected representatives that represent the patients getting service — is not such a bad thing.

RUDYARD GRIFFITHS: Howard, this question is for you. Why do you not take advantage of market forces in terms of allowing for private medicine? Why is the market the big bugaboo for supporters of a single-payer system?

HOWARD DEAN: The market doesn't work in health care. Let me explain why. If a Ford dealer comes into town and there's already another one there, then generally there is going to be some price competition. But if somebody builds a new cardiac catheterization lab, it just gets used a lot more and it costs the system a lot more money.

Let's suppose you're my patient. If I'm a car salesman and you're coming to see me to buy a car, you decide what you want to buy and how much you can afford or if you can afford something at all. But if you come to see me as a patient, I tell you what you are going to buy, I tell you how much it is going to cost, and we send the bill to a third party. There is no relationship of supply and demand in the transaction between doctors and patients.

Secondly, this is a commodity that is essential for life. So even if we were to ration it somehow by price, which is sort of what we do informally, there would be a huge moral component to doing that because then everybody who couldn't afford it would get cut off without health care. Market capitalism doesn't work in health care.

Does that mean it never works? No. There are some areas where it makes some sense. There are little snippets here and there, but this system will never be a real market system. It's why we have this very hybrid way of doing things in America. Ours evolved differently than yours did. I think yours is much more ordered.

In Medicare, 4 percent of money that is given into the system gets spent on administration. The average insurance company pays between 14 percent and 28 percent. There's a ton of money that is spent on bureaucracy. And it's one of the reasons the American system is so much more expensive than yours.

But don't ever let anybody tell you that market capitalism can work in health care. It cannot and it never will and it shouldn't.

WILLIAM FRIST: I think this is an important point because one of the objectives of this debate is to make clear the contrast between the different systems. Markets do work in health care. We need to work towards making them work better in health care, however.

There are a lot of examples that I can give. As a policy example, in 2003, prescription drugs were not a part of our seniors' Medicare program. For 42 million seniors, prescription drugs are probably the most powerful tool in our armamentarium to fight disease. Prescription drugs had been excluded from the Medicare program and in 2003 we put them in, and 42 million people, as part of their basic package, had affordable access to prescription drugs.

We did it because we believe in markets. We did it in such a way that if you have 42 million people, you would have 5 million people competing against 3 million people, competing against 2 million people versus 4 million people, with bargaining, negotiating, and competition on the price of drugs.

That was the first time it had ever been done in our single-payer system. But we are beginning to open up that system to the markets, and with that the cost of prescription drugs — one of the big drivers in health care costs today — has come down 20 percent each year, more than predicted. It was the result of prudent decision-making and trusting individuals to make those decisions rather than a few bureaucrats in Washington, D.C.

For markets to work it goes back to building on what Howard said. You need to have a prudent shopper and you need to have a price and you need to have somebody who is selling something or providing something. And you have to have transparency, full accountability, and understanding of what you are actually buying.

In health care, we, in the U.S. and Canada, have underinvested in information technology. You need to know what's out there. So you ask, how much is that CT scan? How much is that MRI machine? And what are the benefits? We as consumers should decide, not bureaucrats, not politicians in Washington, D.C. And that's a fundamental difference.

In America, we want to be in control and make decisions when it comes to our child with leukemia. We don't want to be told that technology is not the answer. We want the best and we want the transparency to be able to determine that.

And it's not going to be what we heard from Governor Dean during this debate, that waiting times are okay. You would not feel that way if you had a child in that situation. So I believe that markets do work.

One other thing I'd like to mention is that the examples of private sector investment in research, in creativity, and in the new drugs and new devices — and in the CAT scans and CT scans we looked at — are coming predominantly from our private sector. David mentioned that one hospital in the U.S. has a research budget bigger than your entire country. And I know there are ways to explain that, but the U.S. spends 123 billion dollars every year to give you advances, to give you the cures, to give you the new tests, and 60 percent of that comes from the private sector. Forty percent comes from our government.

If you open a bit to the private sector and to competition in this country, if you don't say "no" reflexively, those are the sorts of advantages that you will see across Canada.

RUDYARD GRIFFITHS: This final question is for Robert and David because it's a Canadian question. Do user fees — such as the twenty-five-dollar user fee proposed by the Government of Quebec— help limit waste, abuse, and fraud?

DAVID GRATZER: As a physician and psychiatrist, I'm very conscious about the user fee issue because many of the patients I treat are people who have severe mental illness, for instance, homeless schizophrenics. Obviously you'd never want a user fee for that group. But I think that there are many groups where it would be applicable.

I think in Canada we've been just too unambitious in reaching out to the rest of the world for ideas. In Sweden they have user fees. Many countries have some sort of cost-sharing mechanism. The trouble is that we're not studying our system and saying, where can we find new ideas? We're studying our system through the prism of nationalism. So I like user fees for some people. I like full cost for other people, by the way.

When Conrad Black is finished his jail term, or perhaps if he wins his appeal, he'll come back to Canada and he'll be in his mid-sixties. Prescription drugs will be completely free to him at the point of use. He'll leave his house on the Bridle Path, he'll go to the pharmacy, and he won't pay anything. You'll pay for it. That is an absurdity.

We need to have a mature discussion in Canada about what we're going to cover and how and for whom. I also believe we should be means testing more than prescription drugs.

ROBERT BELL: I don't like user fees for the reasons that David mentioned. Some of the people that need care most are unable to pay user fees, so you start giving in to this terrible health-equity situation. But more important than that, user fees are actually a cop-out. They take our feet away from the fire. If you've got a system that you're worried about in terms of sustainability, why are you looking at bringing more money into it by charging people for access? Why don't you talk about reducing costs and improving quality?

I think user fees are a reflex answer. I don't think they are socially equitable, nor do I think they'll stimulate the kind of innovation that we need.

DAVID GRATZER: That's the problem in Canada. Someone comes up with a perfectly reasonable idea and we immediately shoot it down. If Sweden, the home of social democracy and also eugenics, can embrace this, why can't we even consider it? Sweden is a country where, if you are not feeling well, the government will not only give you short-term disability, they'll send you to the spa for seven weeks. It is a socialist country.

No one is suggesting that this will solve all of our problems. But if it is an idea that they can embrace in Western Europe, we ought to use it here because we're in a real pickle. We will have more elderly people than children over the next five years, and we've got a system that is completely unsustainable and, frankly, not yielding good results. Everything ought to be on the table.

HOWARD DEAN: We debate this internally in the U.S. all the time and I don't have a big problem with user fees, although I think Robert is right, it's a bit of a bureaucratic nightmare. The problem with user fees is that it doesn't do the job. The huge cost increases in the United States are not because of how many times you see your family doctor or even how many prescriptions you get. The enormous cost increases are from how many CT scans, MRIs, and cardiac bypasses we do, and there's not a user fee that's going to deter that.

RUDYARD GRIFFITHS: Well, the time has come for our debaters' closing arguments. I want to call on our debaters in the reverse order of their opening statements, so Governor Dean, you are up first.

HOWARD DEAN: First, let me make this point. I actually think that it is likely — and I saw a poll in the *Globe and Mail* that said that 64 percent of Canadians think this is true — that our two systems are going to show some convergence over the next couple of decades. In fact, Canada may adopt user fees, and the U.S. may adopt a larger form of a single-payer system. So there will be some convergence, but here's what I'd like you to keep in mind as you decide that it is much better to get sick in Canada if you have to get sick.

These are two great countries. At the top end, our medical systems are very good. It's true that we pay for a lot of innovation, but it comes across the border, so it works fine from the point of view of what happens if you get sick in Canada.

The question is, what kind of system do you want to live in? Do you want to live in a system that covers every single citizen of your country, or do you want to live in a system where two thirds of people can get what they need and the others can't? Do you want to live in a system where 18 percent of the gross national product is spent on health care, or do you want to live in a system which also has increasing health care costs — but where only 11 percent is spent on health care?

Your universal health care system is 70 percent cheaper than our system, which isn't universal. Yours is simple. It's easy to understand. Everybody gets coverage. Both of our systems have a lot of problems. The argument that I would leave you with is that for whatever faults that you have in Canada, and there are plenty, you have a system which is coherent, you have a system which is universal, and you have a system which is morally justifiable. We have none of those.

271

If I get sick in the United States, I think I'm going to get pretty good health care. And if you get sick in Canada, you have pretty good health care. The question you have to decide is whether you are going to be one of the 35 percent that can't afford it in the United States or whether you're going to be guaranteed of having that health care. And what you are essentially buying in this country is the notion that no matter what happens to you, your children will not be burdened because of this extraordinary need that all of us have for decent health care.

Most of us will never need to use that much health care in our lifetimes, but we don't know which of us will need that care. In Canada you've done something about that. We have yet to do it.

DAVID GRATZER: Born and raised in Canada, I used to support our system. I thought it was better than the system in the U.S. I believed some of the same arguments you've heard during this debate from our opponents about the Canadian system having better outcomes and at a lower cost. I re-examined things working in hospital rooms and emergency wards. I met people who were waiting for treatment in pain and in fear. It made me rethink everything I thought was important about our health care system.

I did what scientists are supposed to do. I looked for evidence of what was wrong. I discovered our problems were consistent across the system and across the nation. A decade and a half later we are still putting national pride ahead of patient needs. Yes, there are advantages to the Canadian system. Everyday drugs are cheaper. The paperwork is easier.

Doctors can never charge you if you show up to the emergency department with a runny nose.

It's the best health care system in the world as long as you don't get very sick. But when you do, you discover a different system. As if the anxiety and pain of cancer weren't already enough, in a recent survey the Canadian Breast Cancer Network found that eight in ten breast cancer survivors suffered serious financial consequences from their treatment. One in five incurred significant debt in Canada. How could that happen in a country where health care is supposed to be free?

The reason is, we put politics first. The flu shots are free but the PET scans are capped. And the cancer drugs may not even be covered, depending on what a handful of bureaucrats decide. This debate is more complicated than a simple resolution. Tommy Douglas said that we should measure the success of a health care system as a system that keeps people healthy, not just a system that patches them up.

It is true that in both countries we need to improve wellness. But in terms of patching people up when they are sick, which is what the resolution is ultimately about, their system is superior. Study after study says the same thing. Their five-year cancer outcomes are better than ours; the same thing with heart attack and stroke and spinal injuries. And, yes, transplants, too.

Dr. Bell, you had one study, from Johns Hopkins University — an impressive school — but I've taken into account studies from *The Lancet Oncology* and a slew of other journals. You know why the U.S. has better outcomes? Because in the United States they spend more and they're more innovative. In Canada we tend to judge the system by a political standard. But I believe we should measure Canadian health care based on a medical standard.

Too often we fail to deliver the care people need in the medically recommended time. Let me be clear again and say this: the American system is not perfect. We can learn much from that system, but we can learn much from Europe and Asia as well. But the American system is more advanced, delivers timelier care, and if you are ill it is more likely to heal you.

Go back to the resolution. It's not which system is more nationalistically satisfying or which system makes you feel more emotionally well. It is, where would you rather get sick? The answer must be where the outcomes are better — in the United States.

ROBERT BELL: There is a marketplace that determines health care outcomes in Ontario. It's a social marketplace that provides information. You can go find any procedure on the Ontario Wait Times Strategy web site, you can find waiting times for procedures provided across this province in any hospital.

Here's what you'll find: about 3.7 million people are treated and sent home from our emergency departments every year. Nine out of ten of those people have left the hospital within 4.2 hours after they arrived. These figures have improved dramatically over the past three years.

If you're having a heart attack — you can't get sicker than that, referring to David's comment — 90 percent of Toronto patients have their blocked arteries dilated and stented within ninety minutes, a time that saves heart muscle from destruction. The average breast cancer patient in Ontario has completed all tests and had surgery within three weeks, according to the web site. And nine out of ten patients have completed their initial stages of treatment, diagnosis, and surgery within five weeks. As for hip replacement in our hospital, 90 percent of people receive their treatment within three months. Across the province, nine out of ten patients complete the surgery within five months. All the data is there for you to see on the web site — heart treatments, cancer treatments, surgery for all types of disease.

And if you don't like the hospital you have been referred to, you can always look for a different hospital, providing better access to care. Each hospital has provided all their data, and performance has improved dramatically over the last four years.

Remember, as the Governor mentioned, the most dangerous beast in the animal kingdom is a surgeon without a waiting list. If you see a surgeon and they book your surgery for next week — as many of our colleagues south of the border do — then you need to ask yourself: do I need the surgery or does the surgeon need to fill their OR list?

If you're wealthy and you want to pay a premium for immediate access to care, as Danny Williams did, you can get it more readily in America than you can in Canada. However, you are also much more likely to get economically driven unnecessary surgery or treatment in the United States, and with the advent of pay-for-performance, our wait times are shrinking.

There is no question that we need to improve our system. With public accountability through publishing data on web sites, we are now developing a true system where inputs and outputs, including quality, can be measured and improved at a fraction of what you'd pay in America.

Ladies and gentlemen, we are all engaged in a creative, entrepreneurial exercise, designing publicly funded health care which will be cost-effective and high quality for our children and grandchildren. We need to keep our nerve and keep demanding accountability for money and quality, not asking whether or not we have the right system.

WILLIAM FRIST: If your daughter has cancer, you want the best for her and you want it now. You don't want to have decisions made that ultimately reflect back to decisions that were made by a bureaucrat, by a politician, by somebody at the top. And you don't want access to a specialist, the one who has spent his or her lifetime studying leukemia, that cancer that your daughter has, limited by rationing that occurs somewhere far away.

The U.S. system is in need of reform. We made a huge step towards the Canadian ideal of universality earlier this year. But a single-payer, totally funded public system will never be adopted by Americans. Americans by their very nature are much more individualistic, less taken with the European construct of solidarity, more inspired by high — sometimes too high — expectations that for your daughter or your wife, there is going to be the very best care available with medical advances and modern technology, and that they'll have it when it's needed.

In the U.S., in our pluralistic system, we don't see this centralized control which ultimately does create longer wait times. It does force our opponents to make the argument that less technology is good, that in regard to medical advances we should go slowly.

We don't have those upstream limits on physician supply and specialization. We don't have those limits on technology or on capital expenditures. We're not afraid of the private marketplace. We will go there to access capital if it comes down to improving the care of your daughter.

Yes, America has a lot to do to transform its system to a value-based one rather than one based on volume. Individual consumer and employer mandates are a huge advantage for us.

Canadians get good value, but maybe too little is spent. In the United States, when it comes to cancer, if you have prostate cancer or breast cancer the outcomes are better. And if you have cancer you are more likely to have earlier screening and survival if you are in the United States. If you have diabetes diagnosed, you are twice as likely to have begun treatment within six months of having the diagnosis.

Wait times matter. If you need the most modern technology to make a more thorough and a more rapid diagnosis, you would rather be in the United States. So don't get sick. But if you do get sick — and if you get really sick — come and see us in America.

SUMMARY: At evening's start, the pre-debate vote was 23 percent in favour of the resolution and 70 percent against, and 7 percent were undecided. The final vote showed a shift and a disappearance of the undecided voters, with 23 percent in favour of the resolution and 77 percent against.

ACKNOWLEDGEMENTS

The Munk Debates are the product of the public spirited-ness of a remarkable group of civic-minded organizations and individuals. First and foremost, these debates would not be possible without the vision and leadership of the Aurea Foundation. Founded in 2006 by Peter and Melanie Munk, the Aurea Foundation supports Canadian individuals and institutions involved in the study and development of public policy. The debates are the foundation's signature initiative; a model for the kind of substantive public policy conversation Canadians want and need. Since their creation in 2008, the foundation has underwritten the entire cost of each semi-annual event. The debates have also benefitted from the input and advice of members of the board's foundation, including Andrew Coyne, Devon Cross, Margaret MacMillan, Anthony Munk, Nigel Wright, and Janice Gross Stein.

Since their inception the Munk Debates have sought to take the discussions that happen at each event to national and international audiences. Here the debates have benefitted immeasurably from their partnership with Canada's national newspaper the *Globe and Mail* and the counsel of its former editor-in-chief Edward Greenspon. The country's public broadcaster, the CBC, and Executive Producer of CBC Radio's *Ideas*, Bernie Lucht, have created an enthusiastic and growing national radio audience for the debates. The Internet has also played a key role in disseminating the debates. Their online popularity is in large part the result of the expert advice and services of web firm ecentricarts inc. and its principals, Michel Blondeau, Keith Durrant, and Sean Kozey.

With the publication of this superb book, House of Anansi Press is helping the debates reach new audiences in Canada and abroad. The debates' organizers would like to thank Anansi Chairman, Scott Griffin, and President and Publisher, Sarah MacLachlan, for their enthusiasm for this book project and insights into how to translate each spoken debate into a powerful written exchange.

As the moderator of the Munk Debates, I would like to especially thank the Aurea Foundation's Senior Policy Adviser, George Jonas, and its President, Allan Gotlieb. Both have been instrumental in guiding the debates in three short years from a concept into arguably one of Canada's most influential public venues for the discussion of domestic and global public policy issues. Finally, as the co-organizer of the debates with my colleague, Patrick Luciani, I would like to acknowledge the team effort that has driven this initiative since its inception. In this regard, Patrick and I owe a great debt of gratitude to event organizer Deborah Lewis, who spearheaded the early debates. Vital to the debates' continuing success is event manager Sherry Naylor and her entire team at MDG & Associates, and Taylor Owen, our research director.

Rudyard Griffiths
Editor, *The Munk Debates*
Toronto, July 2010

ABOUT THE DEBATERS

DR. ROBERT BELL is President and CEO of University Health Network (UHN). He is an internationally recognized orthopaedic surgeon, health care executive, clinician-scientist, and educator. Dr. Bell was Vice President, Chief Operating Officer of Princess Margaret Hospital and was a Chair of the Clinical Council for Cancer Care Ontario (CCO), as well as a Regional Vice President (Toronto) for CCO from 2003 to 2005. He earned a Doctor of Medicine from McGill University and a Masters of Science from the University of Toronto, and he completed a Fellowship in Orthopaedic Oncology at Massachusetts General Hospital and Harvard University. Dr. Bell is a Fellow of the Royal College of Physicians and Surgeons of Canada, the American College of Surgeons, and the Royal College of Surgeons of Edinburgh.

JOHN BOLTON is a diplomat and lawyer. From June 2001 to May 2005, he served as Under Secretary of State for Arms

Control and International Security. In this role, a key area of his responsibility was the prevention of proliferation of Weapons of Mass Destruction. From 2005 to 2006, he served as the United States Permanent Representative to the UN. He has also held positions as Assistant Secretary for International Organization Affairs at the Department of State; Assistant Attorney General, Department of Justice; Assistant Administrator for Program and Policy Coordination, U.S. Agency for International Development; General-Counsel, U.S. Agency for International Development; and he currently serves as a Senior Fellow at the American Enterprise Institute for Public Policy Research.

PAUL COLLIER is the author of the award-winning book *The Bottom Billion: Why the Poorest Countries Are Failing and What Can Be Done About It.* He is a Professor of Economics at the University of Oxford, Director for the Centre for the Study of African Economics at the University of Oxford, and a Professorial Fellow at St. Anthony's College. He has also served as Senior Adviser to Tony Blair's Commission for Africa, and was Director of the Development Research Group at the World Bank from 1998 to 2003. His most recent book, *The Plundered Planet: Why We Must, and How We Can, Manage Nature for Global Prosperity,* was published in 2010.

DR. HOWARD DEAN is a former Democratic National Committee Chairman, presidential candidate, six-term governor, and physician. He graduated from Yale University with a B.A. in political science, and received his medical degree from the Albert Einstein College of Medicine in New York

City in 1978. After completing his residency at the Medical Center Hospital of Vermont, he went on to practise internal medicine in Shelburne, Vermont. Dean began his career in public service in 1982, when he transitioned from a full-time practising physician to an elected representative in Vermont. He served as Governor of Vermont for twelve years — the second longest serving in the state. Dr. Howard Dean is a CNBC contributor and is the founder of Democracy for America.

HERNANDO DE SOTO is an economist and the international best-selling author of *The Mystery of Capital: Why Capitalism Triumphs in the West and Fails Everywhere Else.* He is President of the Institute for Liberty and Democracy (ILD), and he has served as an economist for the General Agreement on Tariffs and Trade (GATT), as President of the Executive Committee of the Copper Exporting Countries Organization (CIPEC), as CEO of Universal Engineering Corporation, and as a governor of Peru's Central Reserve Bank. He was named as one of the five leading Latin American innovators of the twentieth century by *TIME* magazine.

GARETH EVANS is President and Chief Executive of the International Crisis Group (ICG). He served as a member of the Australian Parliament for twenty-one years, and he is one of Australia's longest serving Foreign Ministers. He was co-chair of the International Commission on Intervention and State Sovereignty (ICISS) in 2000–1, which published its report, *The Responsibility to Protect,* in December 2001. He was a member of the UN Secretary-General's Advisory

Committee on the Prevention of Genocide, and he is currently Co-Chair of the International Advisory Board of the Global Centre for the Responsibility to Protect. He is the award-winning author of several books, including *The Responsibility to Protect: Ending Mass Atrocity Crimes Once and For All*, and he was made an Officer of the Order of Australia in 2001.

MIA FARROW is an award-winning actress and advocate. She has appeared in more than forty films, including *Hannah and Her Sisters*, *The Purple Rose of Cairo*, *Crimes and Misdemeanors*, and *Husbands and Wives*. As an advocate she raises awareness for children's rights in conflict-affected regions, predominantly in Africa. She is a UNICEF Goodwill Ambassador, and has worked extensively to draw attention to the fight to eradicate polio, which she survived as a child. She has visited Darfur and neighbouring countries six times since 2004, and led the effort to focus public attention on China's support for the government of Sudan in the lead-up to the 2008 Olympic Games in Beijing. In 2008, she was named one of the most influential people in the world by *Time* magazine.

NIALL FERGUSON, considered one of the world's leading historians, is the author of several internationally acclaimed works, including *The Pity of War*, *The Cash Nexus: Money and Power in the Modern World*, and *The War of the World: Twentieth-Century Conflict and the Descent of the West*. He is the Laurence A. Tisch Professor of History at Harvard University and William Ziegler Professor of Business Administration at Harvard Business School. He is also a Senior Research Fellow at Jesus College, Oxford University, and a Senior Fellow of the Hoover Institution, Stanford University. He is a prolific commentator on contemporary politics and economics, and he is a contributing editor for the *Financial Times* and a regular contributor to *Newsweek*. In 2004, *TIME* magazine named him one of the world's hundred most influential people.

DR. WILLIAM FRIST is a renowned heart and lung transplant surgeon, and a former U.S. Senate Majority Leader. He is Professor of Business and Medicine at Vanderbilt University. He was the Founder and Director of the Vanderbilt Transplant Center, and he has performed more than 150 heart and lung transplants and authored more than 400 newspaper articles. He is the author of seven books on topics such as bioterrorism, transplantation, and leadership. He is Chair of Save the Children's "Survive to Five Campaign" and Hope Through Healing Hands. Dr. Frist represented Tennessee in the U.S. Senate for twelve years and served on both the Health and Finance committees, which were responsible for writing health legislation. He is considered one of the most influential leaders in American health care.

DR. DAVID GRATZER is a physician and a senior fellow at the Manhattan Institute. He is the author of four books, including *Code Blue: Reviving Canada's Health Care System*, which was awarded the Donner Prize for best Canadian public policy book. His writing has appeared in several publications, including the *Wall Street Journal*, the *Washington Post*, the

Los Angeles Times, and the *Weekly Standard*. Dr. Gratzer has recently been cited in the *New England Journal of Medicine* and *Health Affairs*, as well as by major media outlets across the United States and Canada. He has delivered keynote addresses at several major industry conferences, including the World Health Congress and the [U.S.] National Consumer Driven Health Care Conference. He also testified before Congress on the *Health Care Choice Act*, and was the keynote speaker at the Long Island Health Care Summit.

RICK HILLIER is the former Chief of the Defence Staff for Canadian Forces and a military advocate. He has served throughout Canada, notably commanding the two-brigade commitment to the Red River floodings and the CF commitment to the Quebec Ice Storm. In 1998 General Hillier was appointed as the Canadian Deputy Commanding General of III Armoured Corps, U.S. Army in Fort Hood, Texas. In 2000, he took command of the Multinational Division (Southwest) in Bosnia-Herzegovina. He assumed the duties of Assistant Chief of the Land Staff, and the duties of Chief of the Land Staff. In 2003, General Hillier was selected as the next commander of the NATO-led International Security Assistance Force (ISAF) in Kabul, Afghanistan, leading 6,000 allied soldiers. He retired from the Canadian Forces in July 2008.

RICHARD HOLBROOKE is a diplomat best known as the chief architect of the 1995 Dayton Peace Agreement that ended the war in Bosnia. He is the U.S. Special Representative for Afghanistan and Pakistan, and he served as the U.S.

Ambassador to the UN, where he was also a member of President Bill Clinton's cabinet. He was the Secretary of State for Europe, the U.S. Ambassador to Germany, and the Assistant Secretary of State for East Asian and Pacific Affairs. He is the recipient of numerous awards, and he has received several Nobel Peace Prize nominations for his work on negotiation. Holbrooke has written numerous articles and two books, including *To End a War*, which was a *New York Times* best book. He previously wrote a monthly column for the *Washington Post*.

CHARLES KRAUTHAMMER is a Pulitzer Prize–winning author and commentator, and was named by the *Financial Times* as the most influential commentator in America. He earned degrees at McGill University, Oxford University, and Harvard University, and he served as a resident and chief resident in psychiatry at Massachusetts General Hospital. In 1978, he left the medical practice to direct planning in psychiatric research during the Carter administration. Krauthammer currently writes a syndicated column for the *Washington Post*, and he is a contributing editor to the *Weekly Standard* and the *New Republic*. He is also a weekly panelist on *Inside Washington* and a contributor to FOX News.

LORD NIGEL LAWSON, Baron Lawson of Blaby, is a former president of the British Institute of Energy Economics. He is currently Chairman of Oxford Investment Partners and of Central Europe Trust, an advisory and private equity firm. Lawson had a distinguished career as a journalist before entering the Cabinet in the British Parliament in 1981 as Energy Secretary. In 1983, he began a six-year term as Chancellor of the Exchequer, where he was a key proponent of the Thatcher government's privatization policy. He is the author of several best-selling nonfiction works, including *The View from No.11: Memoirs of a Tory Radical* and *An Appeal to Reason: A Cool Look at Global Warming.*

STEPHEN LEWIS is Chair of the Board of the Stephen Lewis Foundation in Canada and Co-Director of AIDS-Free World in the United States. He was the UN Secretary-General's Special Envoy for HIV/AIDS in Africa from 2001 until 2006. His previous roles also include Canadian Ambassador to the UN and Deputy Executive Director of UNICEF. He was an elected member of the Ontario Legislative Assembly, and in 1970 he became leader of the Ontario New Democratic Party. He is the best-selling author of *Race Against Time,* which won the Canadian Booksellers Association's Libris Award for nonfiction book of the year. He is a Companion of the Order of Canada, Canada's highest honour for lifetime achievement, and was awarded the Pearson Peace Medal in 2004 by the United Nations Association in Canada.

BJØRN LOMBORG is Adjunct Professor at the Copenhagen Business School and the best-selling author of *The Skeptical Environmentalist* and *Cool It: The Skeptical Environmentalist's Guide to Climate Change. TIME* magazine named Lomborg one of the world's 100 most influential people; he was also named one of the 50 people who could save the planet by the *Guardian.* Lomborg's commentaries have appeared regularly in prestigious publications such as the *New York Times*, the *Wall Street Journal*, the *Globe and Mail*, the *Guardian*, the *Sunday Telegraph*, *The Times*, *The Economist*, the *Los Angeles Times*, and the *Boston Globe*. He has appeared on television shows such as *Politically Incorrect*, *60 Minutes*, *Larry King Live*, *20/20*, and *BBC Newsnight* among others.

ELIZABETH MAY is Leader of the Green Party of Canada, and an environmentalist, author, and lawyer. Before winning the leadership in 2006, she was the Executive Director of the Sierra Club of Canada. She is the author of seven books, including *At the Cutting Edge: The Crisis in Canada's Forests*, co-authored with Maude Barlow; *Global Warming for Dummies*, co-authored with Zoe Caron; and most recently *Losing Confidence: Power, Politics and the Crisis in Canadian Democracy*. She is the recipient of many awards, including the United Nations Global 500 Award. She was named one of the world's leading women environmentalists by the United Nations, and was made an Officer of the Order of Canada in 2005.

GEORGE MONBIOT is the author of several best-selling books, including *Heat: How to Stop the Planet Burning*; *The Age of Consent: A Manifesto for a New World Order*, and *Captive State: The Corporate Takeover of Britain*. He has held visiting fellowships or professorships at the universities of Oxford, Bristol (philosophy), Keele, East London (environmental science). In 1995, Nelson Mandela presented him with a United Nations Global 500 Award for outstanding environmental achievement. He has also won the Lloyds National Screen-writing Prize for his screenplay *The Norwegian*, a Sony Award for radio production, the Sir Peter Kent Award, and the OneWorld National Press Award. He currently writes a weekly column for the *Guardian*.

DAMBISA MOYO was born and raised in Lusaka, Zambia. She holds a Doctorate in Economics from Oxford University and a Masters from Harvard University's Kennedy School of Government. She also has an MBA in Finance and a Bachelor of Science (Chemistry) from American University in Washington, D.C. She has held positions as a consultant for the World Bank and at Goldman Sachs. Moyo is a Patron for Absolute Return for Kids (ARK), a children's charity, and serves on the boards of the Lundin Charitable Foundation and Room to Read, a non-profit organization that provides educational opportunities to local communities in the developing world. In 2009, *TIME* magazine named her as one of the world's 100 most influential people.

SAMANTHA POWER is a Pulitzer Prize–winning author, professor, and human rights activist. She was a former foreign policy adviser to Barack Obama, and she is currently the Anna Lindh Professor of Practice of Global Leadership and Public Policy at Harvard's John F. Kennedy School of Government. Her book, *A Problem from Hell: America and the Age of Genocide*, was awarded the Pulitzer Prize, the National Book Critics Circle Award, and the Council on Foreign Relations' Arthur Ross Prize for the best book in U.S. foreign policy. Her *New Yorker* article on the horrors in Darfur, Sudan, won the 2005 National Magazine Award for best reporting. From 1993 to 1996, she covered the wars in the former Yugoslavia as a reporter for the *US News and World Report*, the *Boston Globe*, and *The Economist*.

ABOUT THE MODERATORS

LYSE DOUCET is an award-winning Canadian journalist. She is a regular presenter and foreign correspondent for BBC World Service Radio and BBC World News TV. Doucet joined the BBC in 1983, and she has reported from West Africa, Pakistan, Afghanistan, Iran, and the Middle East. She has covered world events, including the funeral of Yasser Arafat in 2004; the aftermath of the tsunami from Tamil Nadu, India, in 2004; and the war in Iraq in 2003. She was awarded an honorary doctorate in Civil Law from the University of King's College, an honorary Doctor of Laws degree from University College at the University of Toronto, and an honorary Doctor of Letters degree from the University of New Brunswick. She recently won gold for Best News Journalist at the Sony Radio Academy Awards.

RUDYARD GRIFFITHS is a co-host of the Business News Network television show *SqueezePlay* and a columnist for the

National Post. He is the co-director of the Munk Debates and the Salon Speakers Series. He is a co-founder of the Historica-Dominion Institute, Canada's largest history and civics NGO. In 2006, he was named one of Canada's "Top 40 under 40" by the *Globe and Mail.* He is the editor of twelve books on history, politics, and international affairs, and the author of *Who We Are: A Citizen's Manifesto,* which was a *Globe and Mail* Best Book of 2009 and a finalist for the Shaughnessy Cohen Prize for Political Writing. He lives in Toronto.

BRIAN STEWART is one of Canada's most respected television reporters. Beginning in 1971, he hosted the current affairs program *Hourglass,* and soon moved on to reporting on national affairs from Ottawa. A specialist in military and foreign affairs, Stewart reported from overseas for both the CBC and NBC in the 1980s. He received international recognition for his reports on the civil war in Sudan and the Ethiopian famine. Stewart joined the CBC current affairs program *The Journal* in 1987 and *The National* in 1992, and most recently hosted *CBC News: Our World* on CBC Newsworld. He is the recipient of numerous prestigious honours and awards, including a Gemini Award and the Gordon Sinclair Award from the Academy of Canadian Cinema and Television.

ABOUT THE MUNK DEBATES ORGANIZERS

RUDYARD GRIFFITHS is a co-host of the Business News Network television show *SqueezePlay* and a columnist for the *National Post*. He is the co-director of the Munk Debates and the Salon Speakers Series. He is a co-founder of the Historica-Dominion Institute, Canada's largest history and civics NGO. In 2006, he was named one of Canada's "Top 40 under 40" by the *Globe and Mail*. He is the editor of twelve books on history, politics, and international affairs, and the author of *Who We Are: A Citizen's Manifesto*, which was a *Globe and Mail* Best Book of 2009 and a finalist for the Shaughnessy Cohen Prize for Political Writing. He lives in Toronto.

PATRICK LUCIANI is the co-director of the Munk Debates and the Salon Speakers Series. He was a former Executive Director of the Donner Canadian Foundation, and he has authored two books on economic issues. He is also the co-author of *XXL: Obesity and the Limits of Shame* (2011) with Neil Seeman. He lives in Toronto.